HDA
INC.
We're helping design America

Builder's Preferred
HOME PLANS

D1306281

HDA, INC., St. Louis, Missouri

Builder's Preferred Home Plans is a collection of our best-selling easy-to-build home plans, including multi-family, featured in a variety of styles and sizes. A broad assortment is presented to match a wide variety of lifestyles and budgets. Each design features floor plans, a front view of the house, interior square footage of the home, number of bedrooms, baths, garage size and foundation types. All floor plans show room and exterior dimensions.

Technical Specifications - At the time the construction drawings were prepared, every effort was made to ensure that these plans and specifications meet nationally recognized building codes (BOCA, Southern Building Code Congress and others). Because national building codes change or vary from area to area some drawing modifications and/or the assistance of a professional designer or architect may be necessary to comply with your local codes or to accommodate specific building site conditions. We advise you to consult with your local building official for information regarding codes governing your area.

Blueprint Ordering - Fast and Easy - Your ordering is made simple by following the instructions on page 359. See page 354 for more information on which types of blueprint packages are available and how many plan sets to order.

Your Home, Your Way - The blueprints you receive are a master plan for building your new home. They start you on your way to what may well be the most rewarding experience of your life.

Contents

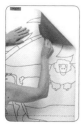  

Making Changes To Your Plan

We understand that it is difficult to find blueprints for a home that will meet all your needs. That is why HDA, Inc. (Home Design Alternatives) is pleased to offer home plan modification services.

Typical home plan modifications include:
- Changing foundation type
- Adding square footage to a plan
- Changing the entry into a garage
- Changing a two-car garage to a three-car garage or making a garage larger
- Redesigning kitchen, baths, and bedrooms
- Changing exterior elevations
- Or most other home plan modifications you may desire!

Some home plan modifications we cannot make include:
- Reversing the plans
- Adapting/engineering plans to meet your local building codes
- Combining parts of two different plans (due to copyright laws)

Our plan modification service is easy to use. Simply:

1. Decide on the modifications you want. For the most accurate quote, be as detailed as possible and refer to rooms in the same manner as the floor plan (i.e. if the floor plan refers to a "den", then use "den" in your description). Including a sketch of the modified floor plan is always helpful.

2. Complete and e-mail the modification request form that can be found online at www.houseplansandmore.com.

3. Within two business days, you will receive your quote. Quotes do not include the cost of the reproducible masters required for our designer to legally make changes.

4. Call to accept the quote and purchase the reproducible masters. For example, if your quote is $850 and the reproducible masters for your plan are $800, your order total will be $1650 plus two shipping and handling charges (one to ship the reproducible masters to our designer and one to ship the modified plans to you).

5. Our designer will send you up to three drafts to verify your initial changes. Extra costs apply after the third draft. If additional changes are made that alter the original request, extra charges may be incurred.

6. Once you approve a draft with the final changes, we then make the changes to the reproducible masters by adding additional sheets. The original reproducible masters (with no changes) plus your new changed sheets will be shipped to you.

Other Important Information:

- Plans cannot be redrawn in reverse format. All modifications will be made to match the reproducible master's original layout. Once you receive the plans, you can make reverse copies at your local blueprint shop.

- Our staff designer will provide the first draft for your review within 4 weeks (plus shipping time) of receiving your order.

- You will receive up to three drafts to review before your original changes are modified. The first draft will totally encompass all modifications based on your original request. Additional changes not included in your original request will be charged separately at an hourly rate of $75 or a flat quoted rate.

- Modifications will be drawn on a separate sheet with the changes shown and a note to see the main sheet for details. For example, a floor plan sheet from the original set (i.e. Sheet 3) would be followed by a new floor plan sheet with changes (i.e. Sheet A-3).

- Plans are drawn to meet national building codes. Modifications will not be drawn to any particular state or county codes, thus we cannot guarantee that the revisions will meet your local building codes. You may be required to have a local architect or designer review the plans in order to have them comply with your state or county building codes.

- Time and cost estimates are good for 90 calendar days.

- All modification requests need to be submitted in writing. Verbal requests will not be accepted.

2 Easy Steps for **FAST** service

1. Visit www.houseplansandmore.com to download the modification request form.

2. E-mail the completed form to customize@hdainc.com or fax to 931-857-7751.

If you are not able to access the internet, please call 1-800-373-2646 (Monday-Friday, 8 - 5 CST).

PLAN DETAILS

- 1,992 total square feet of living area
- Interesting angled walls add drama to many of the living areas including the family room, master bedroom and breakfast area
- Covered porch includes a spa and an outdoor kitchen with sink, refrigerator and cooktop
- Enter the majestic master bath to find a dramatic corner oversized tub
- 4 bedrooms, 3 baths, 2-car side entry garage
- Basement, crawl space or slab foundation, please specify when ordering

BONUS ROOM
10'-7" x 22'-6"

GARAGE
22'-0" x 22'-6"

DECK
24'-8" x 15'-5"

SINK

REFRIG

COOKTOP

HIS

COVERED PORCH
24'-10" x 12'-0"

6' SPA

TV NICHE ABOVE
VENTLESS GAS
FIREPLACE

MECH.

OPTIONAL
STAIRS TO
BASEMENT

SHOWER

SEAT

TRAY CEILING

UP 7

SITTING

CLERESTORY
WINDOW
ABOVE

BREAKFAST
8'-6" x 11'-0"

MASTER BEDROOM
19'-0" x 15'-0"

HERS

19'-3" HIGH CEILING

KITCHEN
17'-3" x 12'-6"

DW

PANT.

FAMILY ROOM
16'-0" x 21'-10"

LINE OF 8'
HIGH CEILING

BEDROOM 2
11'-0" x 14'-0"

OPTIONAL
OPENING FOR
LIVING

LIVING / BEDROOM 3
11'-0" x 12'-0"

OPEN TO
DORMER
ABOVE

DINING
13'-8" x 12'-0"

MEDIA / GUEST ROOM
13'-8" x 11'-0"

PORCH
33'-4" x 6'-0"

62'-0"

66'-2"

PLAN DETAILS

- 1,668 total square feet of living area
- Large bay windows grace the breakfast area, master bedroom and dining room
- Extensive walk-in closets and storage spaces are located throughout the home
- Handy covered entry porch
- Living room has a fireplace, built-in bookshelves and a sloped ceiling
- 3 bedrooms, 2 baths, 2-car drive under garage
- Basement foundation

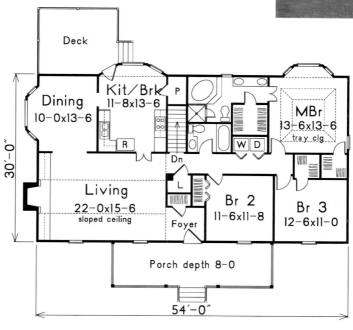

Deck

Dining
10-0x13-6

Kit/Brk
11-8x13-6

P

MBr
13-6x13-6
tray clg

W D

30'-0"

Dn

Living
22-0x15-6
sloped ceiling

L

Br 2
11-6x11-8

Br 3
12-6x11-0

Foyer

Porch depth 8-0

54'-0"

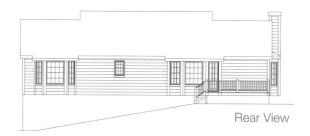

Rear View

PLAN NUMBER: 586-005D-0001

PRICE CODE: B

PLAN DETAILS

- 1,400 total square feet of living area
- Master bedroom is secluded for privacy
- Large utility room has additional cabinet space
- Covered porch provides an outdoor seating area
- Roof dormers add great curb appeal
- Living room and master bedroom feature vaulted ceilings
- Oversized two-car garage has storage space
- 3 bedrooms, 2 baths, 2-car garage
- Basement foundation, drawings also include crawl space foundation

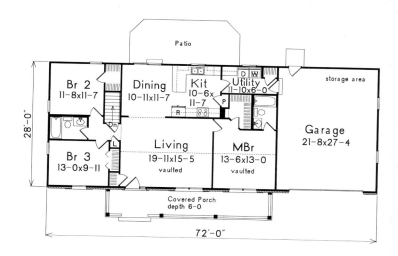

Patio

Br 2
11-8x11-7

Dining
10-11x11-7

Kit
10-6x
11-7

Utility
11-10x6-0

storage area

28'-0"

Dn

Br 3
13-0x9-11

L

Living
19-11x15-5
vaulted

MBr
13-6x13-0
vaulted

D W

P

R

Garage
21-8x27-4

Covered Porch
depth 6-0

72'-0"

Rear View

PLAN DETAILS

- 2,029 total square feet of living area
- Stonework, gables, dormer and double porches enhance facade
- Kitchen has extravagant cabinetry, island snack bar, built-in pantry and dining area with multiple tall windows
- Angled stair descends from large entry with wood columns and is open to a vaulted great room with corner fireplace
- Master bedroom boasts two walk-in closets, a private bath with double-door entry and a secluded porch
- 4 bedrooms, 2 baths, 2-car side entry garage
- Basement foundation, drawings also include crawl space and slab foundations

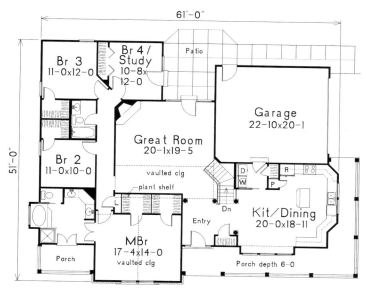

61'-0"

Br 3
11-0x12-0

Br 4 /
Study
10-8x
12-0

Patio

Garage
22-10x20-1

Great Room
20-1x19-5

vaulted clg

plant shelf

Br 2
11-0x10-0

51'-0"

D
W

R

P

Dn

Kit/Dining
20-0x18-11

Entry

MBr
17-4x14-0
vaulted clg

Porch

Porch depth 6-0

Rear View

PLAN DETAILS

- 1,360 total square feet of living area
- Kitchen/dining room features an island workspace and plenty of dining area
- Master bedroom has a large walk-in closet and private bath
- Laundry room is adjacent to the kitchen for easy access
- Convenient workshop in garage
- Large closets in secondary bedrooms maintain organization
- 3 bedrooms, 2 baths, 2-car side entry garage
- Basement foundation, drawings also include crawl space and slab foundations

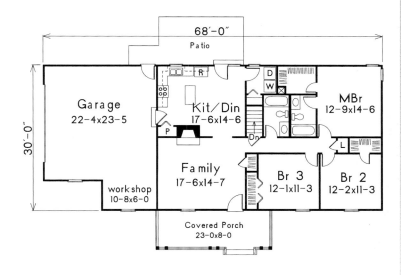

68'-0"

Patio

Garage
22-4x23-5

30'-0"

R

Kit/Din
17-6x14-6

D
W

MBr
12-9x14-6

P

L

Family
17-6x14-7

workshop
10-8x6-0

Br 3
12-1x11-3

Br 2
12-2x11-3

Covered Porch
23-0x8-0

Rear View

PLAN DETAILS

- 1,721 total square feet of living area
- Roof dormers add great curb appeal
- Vaulted dining and great rooms are immersed in light from the atrium window wall
- Breakfast room opens onto the covered porch
- 1,604 square feet on the first floor and 117 square feet on the lower level atrium
- 3 bedrooms, 2 baths, 3-car garage
- Walk-out basement foundation, drawings also include crawl space and slab foundations

Rear View

83'-0"

42'-0"

Covered Porch

Brk
11-5x12-0

Garage
29-4x21-4

Kit
11-5x
12-0

Atrium Below

Dn

Great Rm
16-0x16-10
vaulted

MBr
16-0x14-0
vaulted

vaulted

Dining
11-0x11-6

Br 3
11-1x13-3

Br 2
11-0x12-9

Porch
27-8x5-0

PLAN NUMBER: 586-055D-0017
PRICE CODE: B

PLAN DETAILS

- 1,525 total square feet of living area
- Corner fireplace is highlighted in the great room
- Unique glass block window over the whirlpool tub in the master bath brightens the interior
- Open bar overlooks both the kitchen and great room
- Breakfast room leads to an outdoor grilling and covered porch
- 3 bedrooms, 2 baths, 2-car garage
- Basement, walk-out basement, crawl space or slab foundation, please specify when ordering

51' 6"

GLASS
BLOCKS

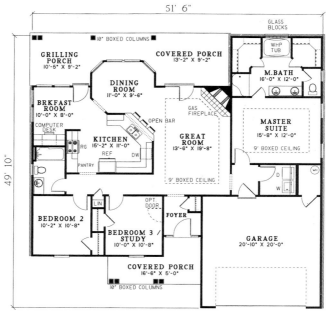

10" BOXED COLUMNS

GRILLING PORCH
10'-6" X 9'-2"

COVERED PORCH
13'-2" X 9'-2"

WHP TUB

M.BATH
16'-0" X 12'-0"

DINING ROOM
11'-0" X 9'-6"

BRKFAST ROOM
10'-0" X 8'-0"

COMPUTER DESK

OPEN BAR

GAS FIREPLACE

MASTER SUITE
15'-8" X 12'-0"

9' BOXED CEILING

KITCHEN
15'-2" X 11'-0"

RG

REF

PANTRY

GREAT ROOM
13'-6" X 19'-8"

49' 10"

9' BOXED CEILING

D

W

WH

LIN

OPT. DOOR

FOYER

BEDROOM 2
10'-2" X 10'-8"

BEDROOM 3 / STUDY
10'-0" X 10'-8"

GARAGE
20'-10" X 20'-0"

COVERED PORCH
16'-6" X 5'-0"

10" BOXED COLUMNS

Rear View

PLAN DETAILS

- 1,501 total square feet of living area
- Spacious kitchen with dining area is open to the outdoors
- Convenient utility room is adjacent to garage
- Master bedroom features a private bath, dressing area and access to the large covered porch
- Large family room creates openness
- 3 bedrooms, 2 baths, 2-car side entry garage
- Basement foundation, drawings also include crawl space and slab foundations

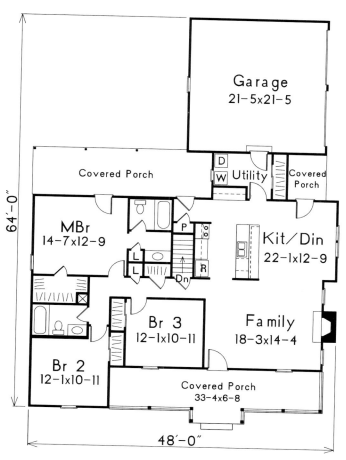

Garage
21-5x21-5

Covered Porch

D

W Utility

Covered
Porch

64'-0"

MBr
14-7x12-9

P

L

L

Dn

R

Kit/Din
22-1x12-9

Br 3
12-1x10-11

Family
18-3x14-4

Br 2
12-1x10-11

Covered Porch
33-4x6-8

48'-0"

PLAN DETAILS

- 1,791 total square feet of living area
- Vaulted great room and octagon-shaped dining area enjoy a spectacular view of the covered patio
- Kitchen features a pass-through to dining area, center island, large walk-in pantry and breakfast room with large bay window
- Master bedroom is vaulted with sitting area
- The garage includes extra storage space
- 4 bedrooms, 2 baths, 2-car garage with storage
- Basement foundation, drawings also include crawl space and slab foundations

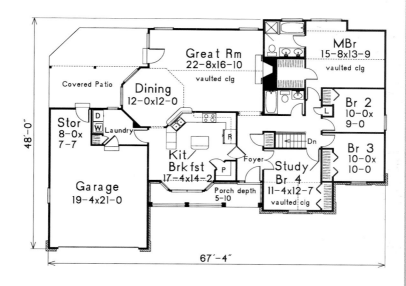

Great Rm
22-8x16-10
vaulted clg

MBr
15-8x13-9
vaulted clg

Covered Patio

Dining
12-0x12-0

Br 2
10-0x
9-0

Stor
8-0x
7-7

D
W
Laundry

Kit/
Brkfst
17-4x14-2

R

L

Br 3
10-0x
10-0

Foyer

Dn

P

Study
Br 4
11-4x12-7
vaulted clg

Garage
19-4x21-0

Porch depth
5-10

48'-0"

67'-4"

Rear View

PLAN DETAILS

- 1,749 total square feet of living area
- Tray ceiling in master suite
- A breakfast bar overlooks the vaulted great room
- Additional bedrooms are located away from the master suite for privacy
- Optional bonus room above the garage has an additional 308 square feet of living area
- 3 bedrooms, 2 baths, 2-car garage
- Slab, crawl space or walk-out basement foundation, please specify when ordering

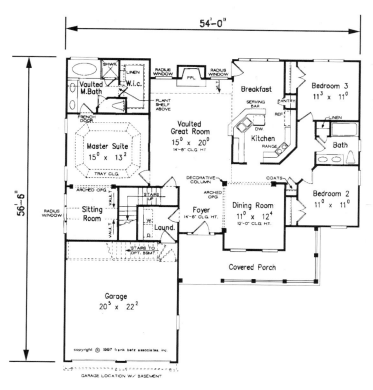

54'-0"

56'-6"

Vaulted M.Bath

SHWR

LINEN

W.i.c.

RADIUS WINDOW

FPL

RADIUS WINDOW

Breakfast

Bedroom 3
11^3 x 11^0

PANTRY

LINEN

FRENCH DOOR

PLANT SHELF ABOVE

SERVING BAR

REF.

Master Suite
15^0 x 13^2

Vaulted Great Room
15^0 x 20^0
14'-8" CLG. HT

Kitchen

DW

RANGE

Bath

TRAY CLG.

DECORATIVE COLUMN

COATS

ARCHED OPG.

STAIRS UP

ARCHED OPG.

Bedroom 2
11^0 x 11^0

RADIUS WINDOW

Sitting Room

W.

Laund.

Foyer
14'-8" CLG. HT.

Dining Room
11^0 x 12^4
12'-0" CLG. HT.

STAIRS TO OPT. BSMT.

Covered Porch

Garage
20^5 x 22^2

copyright © 1997 frank betz associates, inc.

GARAGE LOCATION W/ BASEMENT

PLAN DETAILS

- 1,546 total square feet of living area
- Spacious, open rooms create a casual atmosphere
- Master bedroom is secluded for privacy
- Dining room features a large bay window
- Kitchen and dinette combine for added space and include access to the outdoors
- Large laundry room includes a convenient sink
- 3 bedrooms, 2 baths, 2-car garage
- Basement foundation

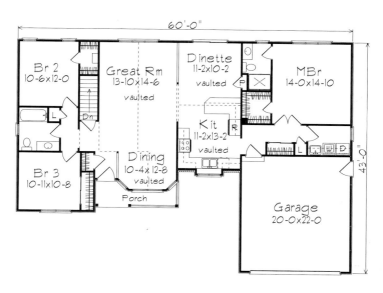

60'-0"

Br 2
10-6x12-0

Great Rm
13-10x14-6
vaulted

Dinette
11-2x10-2
vaulted

MBr
14-0x14-10

Dn

Kit
11-2x13-2
vaulted

R

Dining
10-4x12-8
vaulted

Br 3
10-11x10-8

Porch

Garage
20-0x22-0

43'-0"

Rear View

PLAN NUMBER: 586-007D-0060

PRICE CODE: B

PLAN DETAILS

- 1,268 total square feet of living area
- Multiple gables, large porch and arched windows create a classy exterior
- Innovative design provides openness in the great room, kitchen and breakfast room
- Secondary bedrooms have private hall with bath
- 3 bedrooms, 2 baths, 2-car garage
- Basement foundation, drawings also include crawl space and slab foundations

Rear View

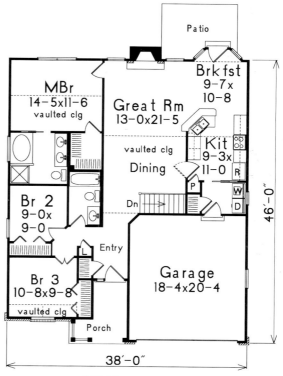

Patio

Brkfst
9-7x
10-8

MBr
14-5x11-6
vaulted clg

Great Rm
13-0x21-5

vaulted clg

Kit
9-3x
11-0

Dining

Br 2
9-0x
9-0

Dn

P

R

W

D

46'-0"

Entry

Br 3
10-8x9-8

vaulted clg

Garage
18-4x20-4

Porch

38'-0"

PLAN DETAILS

- 1,558 total square feet of living area
- The spacious utility room is located conveniently between the garage and kitchen/dining area
- Bedrooms are separated from the living area by a hallway
- Enormous living area with fireplace and vaulted ceiling opens to the kitchen and dining area
- Master bedroom is enhanced with a large bay window, walk-in closet and private bath
- 3 bedrooms, 2 baths, 2-car garage
- Basement foundation

Rear View

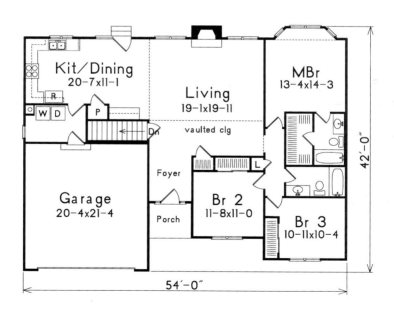

Kit/Dining
20-7x11-1

Living
19-1x19-11

vaulted clg

MBr
13-4x14-3

W D

P

Dn

Garage
20-4x21-4

Foyer

Porch

Br 2
11-8x11-0

Br 3
10-11x10-4

42'-0"

54'-0"

PLAN DETAILS

- 2,193 total square feet of living area
- Master suite includes a sitting room
- Dining room has decorative columns and overlooks family room
- Kitchen has lots of storage
- Optional bonus room with bath on the second floor has an additional 400 square feet of living area
- 3 bedrooms, 3 baths, 2-car side entry garage
- Walk-out basement, crawl space or slab foundation, please specify when ordering

Optional
Second Floor
400 sq. ft.

W.i.c.

Bath

STAIRS DN.

Opt. Bonus
11^0 x 20^0

64'-6"

Bedroom 2
12^1 x 11^6

RADIUS WINDOW

FPL.

RADIUS WINDOW

FRENCH DOOR

PANTRY

TRAY CEILING

Breakfast

DESK

ISLAND

Master Suite
15^0 x 18^0

Sitting Room

Family Room
16^0 x 19^6
13'-5" HIGH CEILING

PASS THRU

D.W.

REF.

PLANT SHELF ABOVE

Bath

LINEN

Kitchen

RANGE

FRENCH DOOR

PLANT SHELF ABOVE

COATS

Laund.

Vaulted
M.Bath

SHWR.

Bedroom 3
10^{10} x 11^0

OPT. DOOR

Foyer
13'-5" HIGH CEILING

W.i.c.

Living Room /
Opt. Bedroom 4
11^0 x 12^2

COVERED ENTRY

Dining Room
12^1 x 12^0
13'-5" HIGH CEILING

W. D.

STAIRS UP

STAIRS TO OPT. BSMT.

Storage

W.S.

LINEN

W.i.c.

59'-0"

First Floor
2,193 sq. ft.

Garage
21^0 x 21^9

copyright © 1995 frank betz associates, inc.

33

PLAN DETAILS

- 1,761 total square feet of living area
- Exterior window dressing, roof dormers and planter boxes provide visual warmth and charm
- Great room boasts a vaulted ceiling, fireplace and opens to a pass-through kitchen
- The vaulted master bedroom includes a luxury bath and walk-in closet
- Home features eight separate closets with an abundance of storage
- 4 bedrooms, 2 baths, 2-car side entry garage
- Basement foundation

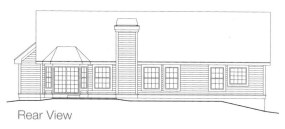

Rear View

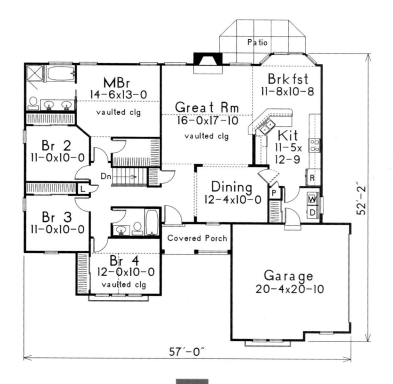

Patio

MBr
14-6x13-0
vaulted clg

Brkfst
11-8x10-8

Great Rm
16-0x17-10
vaulted clg

Kit
11-5x
12-9

Br 2
11-0x10-0

R

Dn

Dining
12-4x10-0

P

W
D

L

Br 3
11-0x10-0

Covered Porch

Br 4
12-0x10-0
vaulted clg

Garage
20-4x20-10

52'-2"

57'-0"

PLAN DETAILS

- 1,708 total square feet of living area
- Massive family room is enhanced with several windows, a fireplace and access to the porch
- Deluxe master bath is accented by a step-up corner tub flanked by double vanities
- Closets throughout maintain organized living
- Bedrooms are isolated from living areas
- 3 bedrooms, 2 baths, 2-car garage
- Basement foundation, drawings also include crawl space foundation

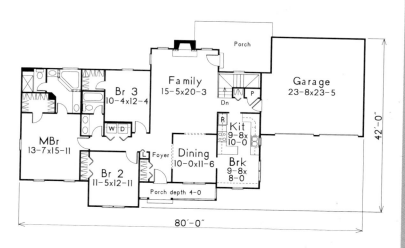

Porch

Family
15-5x20-3

Garage
23-8x23-5

Br 3
10-4x12-4

Dn

P

Kit
9-8x
10-0

MBr
13-7x15-11

W D

R

Foyer

Dining
10-0x11-6

Brk
9-8x
8-0

Br 2
11-5x12-11

Porch depth 4-0

80'-0"

42'-0"

Rear View

PLAN DETAILS

- 1,787 total square feet of living area
- Skylights brighten the screen porch which connects to the family room and deck outdoors
- Master bedroom features a comfortable sitting area, large private bath and direct access to the screen porch
- Kitchen has a serving bar which extends dining into the family room
- 3 bedrooms, 2 baths, 2-car side entry garage
- Basement, crawl space or slab foundation, please specify when ordering

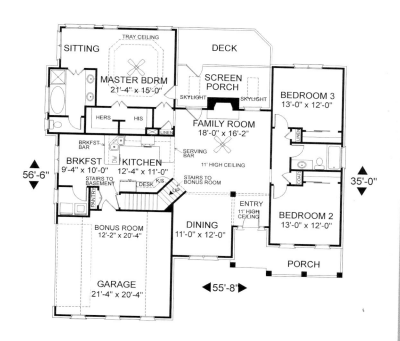

SITTING

TRAY CEILING

MASTER BDRM
21'-4" x 15'-0"

HERS   HIS

BRKFST-
BAR

BRKFST
9'-4" x 10'-0"

KITCHEN
12'-4" x 11'-0"

STAIRS TO
BASEMENT

DESK   K/S

PANTRY

56'-6"

DECK

SCREEN
PORCH

SKYLIGHT   SKYLIGHT

FAMILY ROOM
18'-0" x 16'-2"

LINEN

SERVING
BAR

11' HIGH CEILING

STAIRS TO
BONUS ROOM

UP

DN

BEDROOM 3
13'-0" x 12'-0"

LINEN

COATS

35'-0"

BONUS ROOM
12'-2" x 20'-4"

GARAGE
21'-4" x 20'-4"

DINING
11'-0" x 12'-0"

ENTRY
11' HIGH
CEILING

BEDROOM 2
13'-0" x 12'-0"

PORCH

55'-8"

PLAN DETAILS

- 1,384 total square feet of living area
- Wrap-around country porch for peaceful evenings
- Vaulted great room enjoys a large bay window, stone fireplace, pass-through kitchen and awesome rear views through an atrium window wall
- Master bedroom features a double-door entry, walk-in closet and a fabulous bath
- Atrium opens to 611 square feet of optional living area below
- 2 bedrooms, 2 baths, 1-car side entry garage
- Walk-out basement foundation

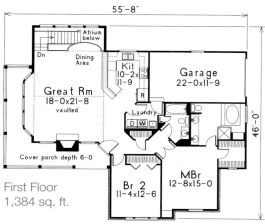

55'-8"

Atrium below

Dn

Dining Area

Kit
10-2x
11-9

Garage
22-0x11-9

Great Rm
18-0x21-8
vaulted

R

Laundry

D W

46'-0"

Cover porch depth 6-0

MBr
12-8x15-0

Br 2
11-4x12-6

First Floor
1,384 sq. ft.

Up

Patio

Family Rm
25-0x21-4

Unexcavated

Unfinished Basement

Optional
Lower Level
611 sq. ft.

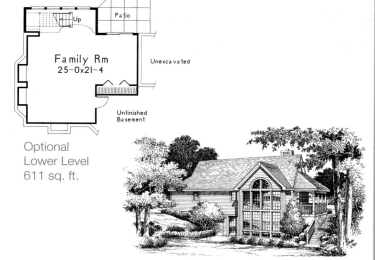

Rear View

PLAN DETAILS

- 1,915 total square feet of living area
- Large breakfast area overlooks the vaulted great room
- Master suite has a cheerful sitting room and private bath
- Plan features a unique in-law suite with private bath and walk-in closet
- 4 bedrooms, 3 baths, 2-car garage
- Walk-out basement, slab or crawl space foundation, please specify when ordering

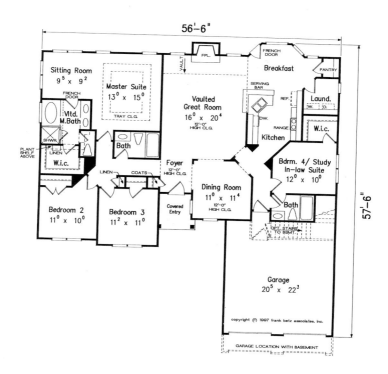

56'-6"

57'-6"

Sitting Room
9⁵ x 9²

Master Suite
13⁰ x 15⁰
TRAY CLG.

FRENCH
DOOR

Vtd.
M.Bath

SHWR.

PLANT
SHELF
ABOVE

LINEN

W.i.c.

Bath

Foyer
12'-0"
HIGH CLG.

LINEN

COATS

Bedroom 2
11⁰ x 10⁰

Bedroom 3
11² x 11⁰

Covered
Entry

FPL.

VAULT.

FRENCH
DOOR

Breakfast

PANTRY

SERVING
BAR

Vaulted
Great Room
16⁰ x 20⁴
12'-0"
HIGH CLG.

REF.

DW.

Laund.

W.

D.

RANGE

Kitchen

W.i.c.

Bdrm. 4/ Study
In-law Suite
12⁰ x 10⁰

Dining Room
11⁰ x 11⁴
12'-0"
HIGH CLG.

Bath

OPT. STAIRS
TO BSMT.

Garage
20⁵ x 22³

copyright © 1997 frank betz associates, inc.

GARAGE LOCATION WITH BASEMENT

PLAN DETAILS

- 2,097 total square feet of living area
- Angled kitchen, family room and eating area add interest to this home
- Family room includes a TV niche making this a cozy place to relax
- Sumptuous master bedroom includes a sitting area, double walk-in closet and a full bath with double vanities
- Bonus room above garage has an additional 452 square feet of living space
- 3 bedrooms, 3 baths, 3-car side entry garage
- Crawl space or slab foundation, please specify when ordering

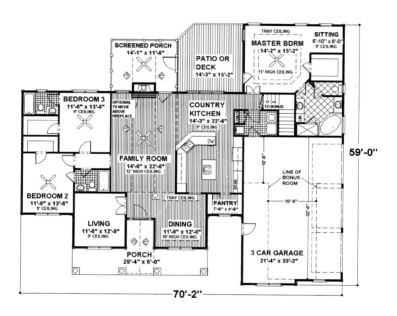

SCREENED PORCH
14'-1" x 11'-6"

PATIO OR DECK
14'-3" x 15'-2"

TRAY CEILING

MASTER BDRM
14'-2" x 15'-2"

11' HIGH CEILING

SITTING
6'-10" x 6'-0"
9' CEILING

BEDROOM 3
11'-0" x 13'-6"
9' CEILING

OPTIONAL
TV NICHE
ABOVE
FIREPLACE

COUNTRY KITCHEN
14'-3" x 22'-6"
9' CEILING

UP
TO BONUS

DW

FAMILY ROOM
14'-0" x 22'-6"
12' HIGH CEILING

DESK

LINE OF
BONUS
ROOM

10'-6"

BEDROOM 2
11'-0" x 13'-6"
9' CEILING

TRAY CEILING

PANTRY
7'-6" x 4'-6"

LIVING
11'-0" x 12'-0"
9' CEILING

DINING
11'-0" x 12'-0"
10' HIGH CEILING

PORCH
29'-4" x 6'-0"

10'-6"

3 CAR GARAGE
21'-4" x 33'-2"

32'-0"

59'-0"

70'-2"

45

PLAN DETAILS

- 2,397 total square feet of living area
- Entry porch leads to a vaulted foyer with plant shelf open to the great room
- The great room enjoys a 12' vaulted ceiling, atrium featuring 2 1/2 story windows and fireplace with flanking bookshelves
- The sunroom and side porch adjoin the breakfast room and garage
- 898 square feet of optional living area on the lower level with family room, bedroom #4 and bath
- 3 bedrooms, 2 baths, 3-car side entry garage
- Walk-out basement foundation

First Floor
2,397 sq. ft.

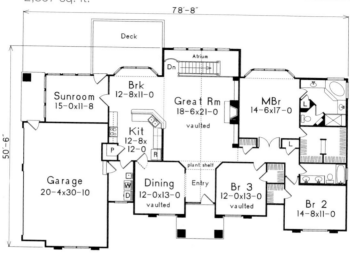

78'-8"

Deck

Atrium

Dn

Sunroom
15-0x11-8

Brk
12-8x11-0

Great Rm
18-6x21-0
vaulted

MBr
14-6x17-0

L

Kit
12-8x
12-0

P

R

plant shelf

50'-6"

Garage
20-4x30-10

W
D

Dining
12-0x13-0
vaulted

Entry

Br 3
12-0x13-0
vaulted

L

Br 2
14-8x11-0

Optional
Lower Level
898 sq. ft.

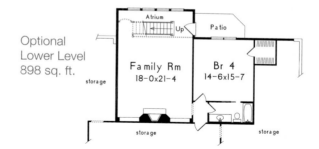

Atrium

Up

Patio

Family Rm
18-0x21-4

storage

Br 4
14-6x15-7

storage

storage

47

PLAN DETAILS

- 1,779 total square feet of living area
- Well-designed floor plan has a vaulted family room with fireplace and access to the outdoors
- Decorative columns separate the dining area from the foyer
- A vaulted ceiling adds spaciousness in the master bath that also features a walk-in closet
- 3 bedrooms, 2 baths, 2-car garage
- Walk-out basement, slab or crawl space foundation, please specify when ordering

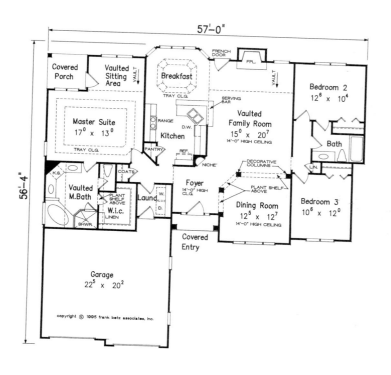

57'-0"

Covered Porch

Vaulted Sitting Area

VAULT

Breakfast

TRAY CLG.

FRENCH DOOR

FPL.

VAULT

Bedroom 2
12⁶ x 10⁴

Master Suite
17⁰ x 13⁰

TRAY CLG.

RANGE

D.W.

Kitchen

PANTRY

REF.

SERVING BAR

Vaulted Family Room
15⁰ x 20⁷
14'-0" HIGH CEILING

NICHE'

Bath

K.B.

Vaulted M.Bath

PLANT SHELF ABOVE

W.i.c.

LINEN

SHWR.

COATS

W.

Laund

D.

Foyer
14'-0" HIGH CLG.

DECORATIVE COLUMNS

PLANT SHELF ABOVE

LIN.

Bedroom 3
10⁶ x 12⁰

Dining Room
12⁵ x 12⁷
14'-0" HIGH CEILING

Covered Entry

Garage
22⁵ x 20²

copyright © 1995 frank betz associates, inc.

56'-4"

PLAN NUMBER: 586-048D-0011

PRICE CODE: B

PLAN DETAILS

- 1,550 total square feet of living area
- Alcove in the family room can be used as a cozy corner fireplace or as a media center
- Master bedroom features a large walk-in closet, skylight and separate tub and shower
- Convenient laundry closet
- Kitchen with pantry and breakfast bar connects to the family room
- Family room and master bedroom access the covered patio
- 3 bedrooms, 2 baths, 2-car garage
- Slab foundation

Rear View

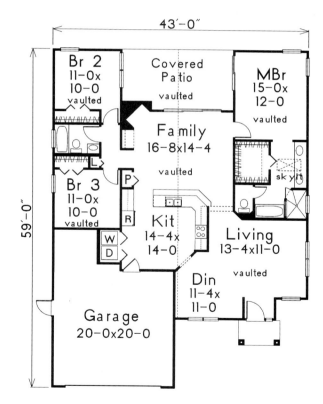

43'-0"

59'-0"

Br 2
11-0x
10-0
vaulted

Covered
Patio
vaulted

MBr
15-0x
12-0
vaulted

Family
16-8x14-4
vaulted

Br 3
11-0x
10-0
vaulted

P

R

W
D

Kit
14-4x
14-0

Living
13-4x11-0

Din
11-4x
11-0

vaulted

sk y lt

Garage
20-0x20-0

PLAN DETAILS

- 1,977 total square feet of living area
- Classic traditional exterior is always in style
- Spacious great room boasts a vaulted ceiling, dining area, atrium with elegant staircase and feature windows
- Atrium opens to 1,416 square feet of optional living area below which consists of a family room, two bedrooms, two baths and a study
- 4 bedrooms, 2 1/2 baths, 3-car side entry garage
- Walk-out basement foundation

76'-0"

45'-0"

MBr
14-6x15-5

open to below   Dn

Brk
11-8x13-0

Deck

Great Rm
16-4x24-2
vaulted

Kit
11-3x
12-4

Br 2
10-7x
10-0

Dining

Garage
23-4x29-4

Br 3
11-4x11x8

Br 4
11-8x12-8
vaulted

Porch

First Floor
1,977 sq. ft.

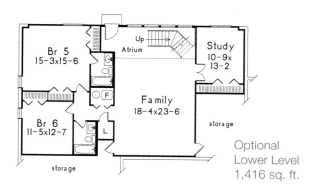

Up
Atrium

Study
10-9x
13-2

Br 5
15-3x15-6

Family
18-4x23-6

storage

Br 6
11-5x12-7

storage

Optional
Lower Level
1,416 sq. ft.

PLAN DETAILS

- 2,322 total square feet of living area
- Vaulted family room has a fireplace and access to the kitchen
- Decorative columns and arched openings surround the dining area
- Master suite has a sitting room and grand-scale bath
- Kitchen includes an island with serving bar
- 3 bedrooms, 2 1/2 baths, 2-car side entry garage
- Walk-out basement, crawl space or slab foundation, please specify when ordering

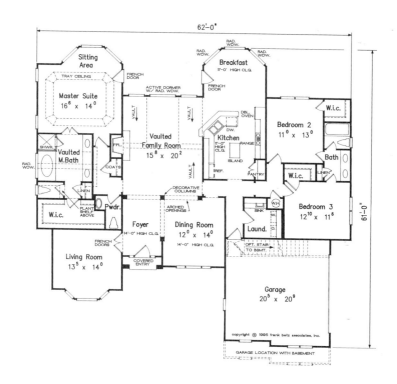

62'-0"

Sitting Area
TRAY CEILING

FRENCH DOOR

Master Suite
16⁸ x 14⁰

RAD. WDW.

RAD. WDW.

RAD. WDW.

Breakfast
11'-0" HIGH CLG.

FRENCH DOOR

ACTIVE DORMER W/ RAD. WDW.

VAULT

VAULT

Vaulted Family Room
15⁸ x 20²

Kitchen
11'-0" HIGH CLG.

DBL. OVEN

DW.

RANGE

ISLAND

REF.

W.i.c.

Bedroom 2
11⁰ x 13⁰

Bath

SHWR.

Vaulted M.Bath

RAD. WDW.

FPL.

COATS

LINEN

VAULT

PANTRY

W.i.c.

LINEN

W.i.c.

PLANT SHELF ABOVE

Pwdr.

DECORATIVE COLUMNS

ARCHED OPENINGS

SINK

W.H.

Laund.

Bedroom 3
12¹⁰ x 11⁸

Foyer
14'-0" HIGH CLG.

Dining Room
12⁰ x 14⁰
14'-0" HIGH CLG.

OPT. STAIR TO BSMT.

FRENCH DOORS

Living Room
13⁵ x 14⁰

COVERED ENTRY

Garage
20⁵ x 20⁹

61'-0"

copyright © 1995 frank betz associates, inc.

GARAGE LOCATION WITH BASEMENT

PLAN DETAILS

- 1,285 total square feet of living area
- Accommodating home with ranch-style porch
- Large storage area on back of home
- Master bedroom includes dressing area, private bath and built-in bookcase
- Kitchen features pantry, breakfast bar and complete view to the dining room
- 3 bedrooms, 2 baths
- Crawl space foundation, drawings also include basement and slab foundations

Rear View

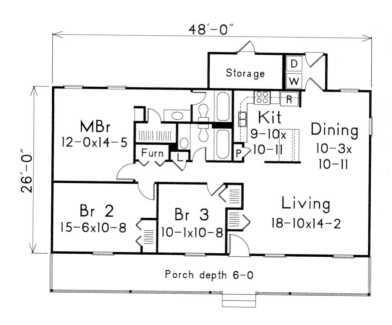

48'-0"

26'-0"

Storage

D
W

MBr
12-0x14-5

Furn   L

Kit
9-10x
10-11

R

P

Dining
10-3x
10-11

Br 2
15-6x10-8

Br 3
10-1x10-8

Living
18-10x14-2

Porch depth 6-0

PLAN DETAILS

- 1,575 total square feet of living area
- Inviting porch leads to spacious living and dining rooms
- Kitchen with corner windows features an island snack bar, attractive breakfast room bay, convenient laundry area and built-in pantry
- A luxury bath and walk-in closet adorn the master bedroom suite
- 3 bedrooms, 2 1/2 baths, 2-car garage
- Basement foundation, drawings also include crawl space and slab foundations

Second Floor
773 sq. ft.

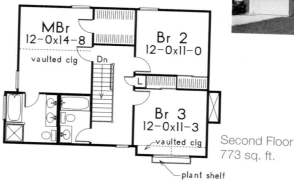

MBr
12-0x14-8

vaulted clg

Dn

Br 2
12-0x11-0

L

Br 3
12-0x11-3

vaulted clg

plant shelf

36'-0"

46'-8"

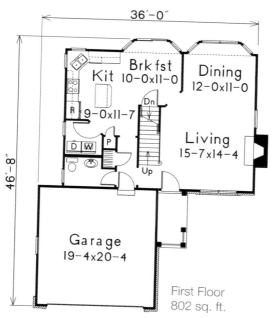

Kit
9-0x11-7

Brkfst
10-0x11-0

Dining
12-0x11-0

Dn

R

D W P

Up

Living
15-7x14-4

Garage
19-4x20-4

First Floor
802 sq. ft.

PLAN DETAILS

- 1,856 total square feet of living area
- Beautiful covered porch creates a Southern accent
- Kitchen has an organized feel with lots of cabinetry
- Large foyer has a grand entrance and leads into the family room through columns and an arched opening
- 3 bedrooms, 2 baths, 2-car side entry garage
- Walk-out basement, crawl space or slab foundation, please specify when ordering

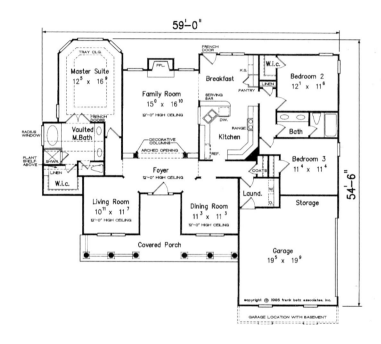

59'-0"

54'-6"

TRAY CLG.

Master Suite
12⁵ x 16⁹

FPL.

Family Room
15⁰ x 16¹⁰
12'-0" HIGH CEILING

FRENCH
DOOR

Breakfast

K.S.

W.i.c.

LINEN

PANTRY

Bedroom 2
12¹ x 11⁶

SERVING
BAR

RADIUS
WINDOW

Vaulted
M.Bath

FRENCH
DOORS

DECORATIVE
COLUMNS

ARCHED OPENING

DW.

RANGE

Kitchen

Bath

PLANT
SHELF
ABOVE

SHWR.

LINEN

REF.

Bedroom 3
11⁴ x 11⁴

W.i.c.

Foyer
12'-0" HIGH CEILING

COATS

Living Room
10¹¹ x 11⁷
12'-0" HIGH CEILING

Dining Room
11³ x 11³
12'-0" HIGH CEILING

Laund.

W.

D.

Storage

Covered Porch

Garage
19⁵ x 19⁹

copyright © 1995 frank betz associates, inc.

GARAGE LOCATION WITH BASEMENT

PLAN DETAILS

- 1,170 total square feet of living area
- Master bedroom enjoys privacy at the rear of this home
- Kitchen has an angled bar that overlooks the great room and breakfast area
- Living areas combine to create a greater sense of spaciousness
- Great room has a cozy fireplace
- 3 bedrooms, 2 baths, 2-car garage
- Slab foundation

Rear View

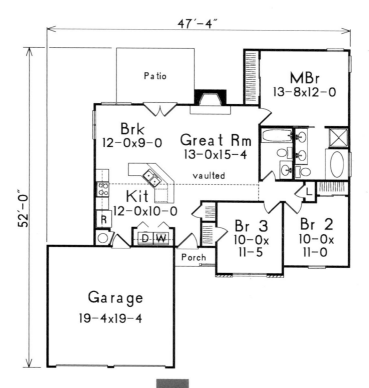

47'-4"

Patio

MBr
13-8x12-0

Brk
12-0x9-0

Great Rm
13-0x15-4

vaulted

Kit
12-0x10-0

L

52'-0"

Br 3
10-0x
11-5

Br 2
10-0x
11-0

R

D W

Porch

Garage
19-4x19-4

PLAN DETAILS

- 1,191 total square feet of living area
- Energy efficient home with 2" x 6" exterior walls
- Master bedroom is located near living areas for maximum convenience
- Living room has a cathedral ceiling and stone fireplace
- 3 bedrooms, 2 baths, 2-car side entry garage
- Slab foundation, drawings also include crawl space foundation

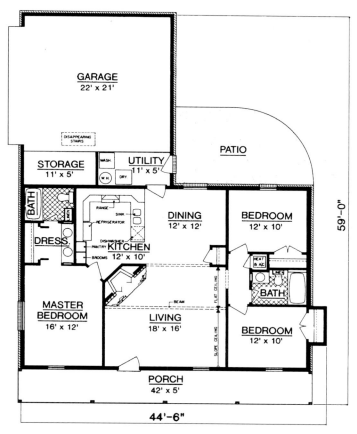

GARAGE
22' x 21'

DISAPPEARING STAIRS

STORAGE
11' x 5'

WASH

W.H. DRY

UTILITY
11' x 5'

PATIO

BATH

RANGE

SINK

REFRIGERATOR

DISHWASHER

PANTRY

BROOMS

DRESS.

KITCHEN
12' x 10'

DINING
12' x 12'

BEDROOM
12' x 10'

HEAT & AC

LINEN

FLAT CEILING

SLOPE CEILING

BATH

MASTER BEDROOM
16' x 12'

BEAM

LIVING
18' x 16'

BEDROOM
12' x 10'

PORCH
42' x 5'

59'-0"

44'-6"

PLAN DETAILS

- 2,107 total square feet of living area
- Master bedroom is separate from other bedrooms for privacy
- Spacious breakfast room and kitchen include center island with eating space
- Centralized great room has fireplace and easy access to any area in the home
- 4 bedrooms, 2 1/2 baths, 2-car garage
- Crawl space, basement, walk-out basement or slab foundation, please specify when ordering

64' 8"

62' 1"

GLASS BLOCKS

WHP TUB

M. BATH

PATIO

COVERED PORCH
31'-8" X 9'-0"

M. BED RM.
16'-8" X 14'-0"
9' PAN CEILING

BED RM. 4
14'-4" X 11'-0"

BRKFST. RM.
12'-6" X 9'-6"

KITCHEN
12'-6" X 10'-0"
REF   PAN

LAU.
W

BATH

GREAT RM.
19'-8" X 17'-0"
10' CEILING

1/2
B.

OVEN   CT.

HVAC   WD

STOR.

BUILT-INS
(OPT TO STUDY)

DW

BED RM. 3
10'-6" X 12'-0"

FOYER
10' CEILING

OPT.
DOOR

DINING RM.
11'-0" X 12'-0"
9' CEILING

GARAGE
20'-4" X 21'-0"

BED RM. 2 /
STUDY
11'-0" X 12'-0"

PORCH

8' CEILING

PLANTER

PLAN DETAILS

- 1,882 total square feet of living area
- Wide, handsome entrance opens to the vaulted great room with fireplace
- Living and dining areas are conveniently joined but still allow privacy
- Private covered porch extends breakfast area
- Practical passageway runs through the laundry room from the garage to the kitchen
- Vaulted ceiling in master bedroom
- 3 bedrooms, 2 baths, 2-car garage
- Basement foundation

Rear View

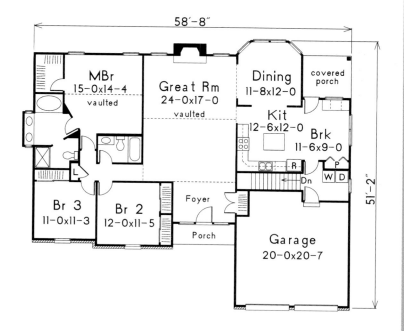

58'-8"

| MBr
15-0x14-4
vaulted | Great Rm
24-0x17-0
vaulted | Dining
11-8x12-0 | covered
porch |

Kit
12-6x12-0

Brk
11-6x9-0

L

Br 3
11-0x11-3

Br 2
12-0x11-5

Foyer

R

Dn

P

W D

51'-2"

Porch

Garage
20-0x20-7

PLAN DETAILS

- 1,140 total square feet of living area
- Open and spacious living and dining areas for family gatherings
- Well-organized kitchen has an abundance of cabinetry and a built-in pantry
- Roomy master bath features a double-bowl vanity
- 3 bedrooms, 2 baths, 2-car drive under garage
- Basement foundation

Rear View

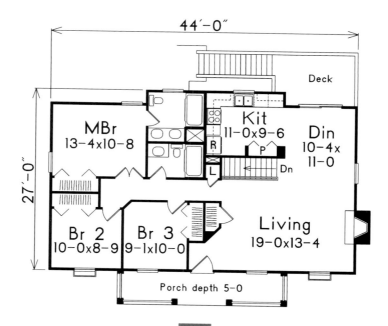

44'-0"

Deck

27'-0"

MBr
13-4x10-8

Kit
11-0x9-6

Din
10-4x
11-0

R

P

Dn

L

Br 2
10-0x8-9

Br 3
9-1x10-0

Living
19-0x13-4

Porch depth 5-0

PLAN DETAILS

- 1,220 total square feet of living area
- Vaulted ceilings add luxury to the living room and master bedroom
- Spacious living room is accented with a large fireplace and hearth
- Dining area is adjacent to the convenient wrap-around kitchen
- Washer and dryer are handy to the bedrooms
- Covered porch entry adds appeal
- Rear deck adjoins dining area
- 3 bedrooms, 2 baths, 2-car drive under garage
- Basement foundation

Rear View

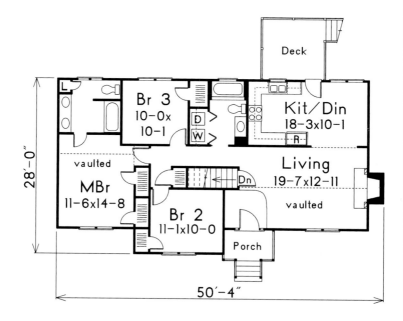

Deck

L

Br 3
10-0x
10-1

D

W

Kit/Din
18-3x10-1

R

vaulted

MBr
11-6x14-8

Dn

Living
19-7x12-11

vaulted

Br 2
11-1x10-0

Porch

28'-0"

50'-4"

PLAN DETAILS

- 1,664 total square feet of living area
- L-shaped country kitchen includes pantry and cozy breakfast area
- Bedrooms are located on the second floor for privacy
- Master bedroom includes a walk-in closet, dressing area and bath
- 3 bedrooms, 2 1/2 baths, 2-car garage
- Crawl space foundation, drawings also include basement and slab foundations

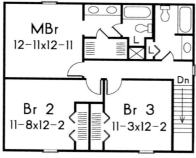

MBr
12-11x12-11

Br 2
11-8x12-2

Br 3
11-3x12-2

Dn

Second Floor
832 sq. ft.

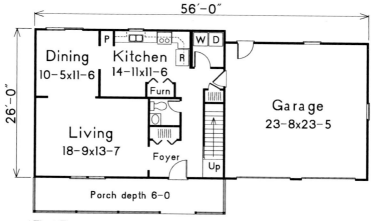

56'-0"

26'-0"

P

Dining
10-5x11-6

Kitchen
14-11x11-6

W   D

R

Furn

Living
18-9x13-7

Foyer

Up

Garage
23-8x23-5

Porch depth 6-0

First Floor
832 sq. ft.

PLAN DETAILS

- 2,126 total square feet of living area
- Kitchen overlooks vaulted family room with a handy serving bar
- Two-story foyer creates an airy feeling
- Second floor includes an optional bonus room with an additional 251 square feet of living area
- 4 bedrooms, 3 baths, 2-car side entry garage
- Walk-out basement, crawl space or slab foundation, please specify when ordering

Second Floor
543 sq. ft.

Attic

Family Room Below

Bath

Bedroom 4
12⁸ x 12⁰

W.i.c.

LINEN

VAULT

OPEN RAIL

STAIRS DN.

OPEN RAIL

OVERLOOK

W.i.c.

W.i.c.

Foyer Below

Bedroom 3
11⁰ x 10⁸

Opt. Bonus Room
11⁵ x 19²

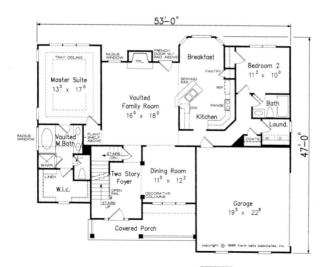

First Floor
1,583 sq. ft.

53'-0"

47'-0"

TRAY CEILING

Master Suite
13⁰ x 17⁰

RADIUS WINDOW

FPL

FRENCH DOOR W/ RAD. ABOVE

Breakfast

Bedroom 2
11² x 10⁰

PANTRY

Vaulted Family Room
16⁰ x 18⁰

SERVING BAR

REF.

RANGE

DW.

Kitchen

Bath

Laund.

RADIUS WINDOW

Vaulted M.Bath

PLANT SHELF ABOVE

COATS

W. D.

SHWR.

LINEN

STAIRS DN.

W.i.c.

Two Story Foyer

Dining Room
11⁰ x 12²

OPEN RAIL

STAIRS UP

DECORATIVE COLUMNS

Garage
19⁵ x 22⁸

Covered Porch

copyright © 1996 frank betz associates, inc.

PLAN DETAILS

- 2,505 total square feet of living area
- The garage features extra storage area and ample workspace
- Laundry room is accessible from the garage and the outdoors
- Deluxe raised tub and immense walk-in closet grace the master bath
- 3 bedrooms, 2 1/2 baths, 2-car side entry garage
- Basement foundation, drawings also include crawl space foundation

Second Floor
1,069 sq. ft.

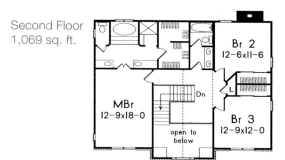

Br 2
12-6x11-6

MBr
12-9x18-0

Dn

L

open to below

Br 3
12-9x12-0

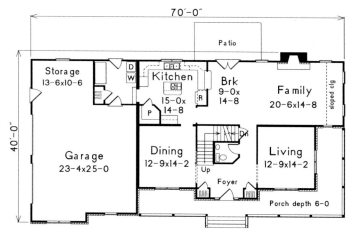

70'-0"

Patio

Storage
13-6x10-6

D
W

Kitchen
15-0x
14-8

R

P

Brk
9-0x
14-8

Family
20-6x14-8

sloped clg

40'-0"

Garage
23-4x25-0

Dining
12-9x14-2

Up

Dn

Living
12-9x14-2

Foyer

Porch depth 6-0

First Floor
1,436 sq. ft.

PLAN DETAILS

- 1,320 total square feet of living area
- Functional U-shaped kitchen features pantry
- Large living and dining areas join to create an open atmosphere
- Secluded master bedroom includes private full bath
- Covered front porch opens into large living area with convenient coat closet
- Utility/laundry room is located near the kitchen
- 3 bedrooms, 2 baths
- Crawl space foundation

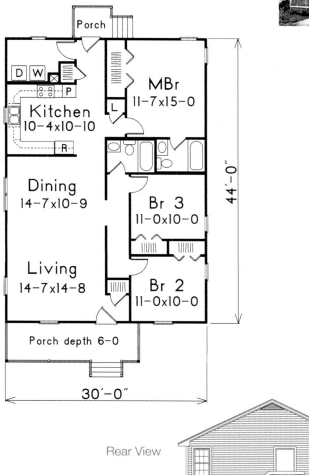

Porch

D W ☐ ☐

Kitchen
10-4x10-10

P

R

MBr
11-7x15-0

L

Dining
14-7x10-9

Br 3
11-0x10-0

Living
14-7x14-8

Br 2
11-0x10-0

Porch depth 6-0

44'-0"

30'-0"

Rear View

PLAN DETAILS

- 1,342 total square feet of living area
- 9' ceilings throughout the home
- Master suite has a tray ceiling and wall of windows that overlooks the backyard
- Dining room includes a serving bar connecting it to the kitchen and sliding glass doors that lead outdoors
- Optional second floor has an additional 350 square feet of living area
- 3 bedrooms, 2 baths, 2-car garage
- Slab, walk-out basement or crawl space foundation, please specify when ordering

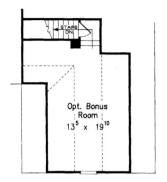

Opt. Bonus Room
13^5 x 19^{10}

Optional
Second Floor
350 sq. ft.

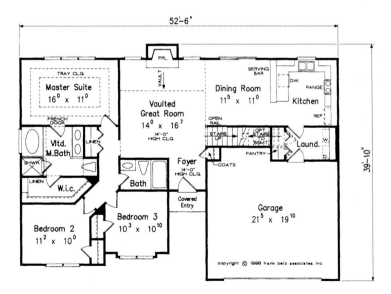

52'-6"

TRAY CLG.

Master Suite
16^0 x 11^0

FRENCH DOOR

Vltd.
M.Bath

LINEN

SHWR

LINEN

W.i.c.

Bedroom 2
11^2 x 10^0

FPL

VAULT

Vaulted
Great Room
14^0 x 16^7
14'-0"
HIGH CLG.

Bath

Bedroom 3
10^3 x 10^{10}

Foyer
14'-0"
HIGH CLG.

Covered
Entry

Dining Room
11^5 x 11^0

SERVING BAR

DW.

RANGE

Kitchen

REF.

OPEN RAIL

STAIRS UP

OPT. STAIRS TO BSMT.

PANTRY

COATS

Laund.

W.

D.

Garage
21^5 x 19^{10}

39'-10"

copyright © 1998 frank betz associates, inc.

First Floor
1,342 sq. ft.

83

PLAN DETAILS

- 1,593 total square feet of living area
- The rear porch is a pleasant surprise and perfect for enjoying the outdoors
- Great room is filled with extras like a corner fireplace, sloping ceiling and view to the outdoors
- A large island with seating separates the kitchen from the dining area
- 3 bedrooms, 2 baths, 2-car garage
- Basement foundation

Dining
12'4" x 12'

Porch
11'4" x 10'9"

Master Bedroom
15'3" x 12

9' ceiling height

Great Room
18'2" x 17'

Kitchen
17'4" x 9'6"

Storage
7' x 14'8"

pantry

Bath

Hall

walk-in
closet

Bath

Foyer

Laun.

Two-car Garage
20' x 22'

Bedroom
11' x 10'2"

Bedroom
10'6" x 11'

Porch

slope
ceiling

slope
ceiling

48'10"

60'

PLAN DETAILS

- 864 total square feet of living area
- L-shaped kitchen with convenient pantry is adjacent to dining area
- Easy access to laundry area, linen closet and storage closet
- Both bedrooms include ample closet space
- 2 bedrooms, 1 bath
- Crawl space foundation, drawings also include basement and slab foundations

Rear View

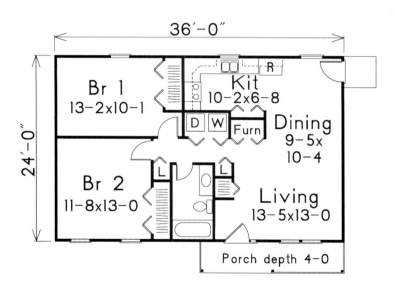

36'-0"

24'-0"

Br 1
13-2x10-1

Kit
10-2x6-8

R

Dining
9-5x
10-4

D W Furn

Br 2
11-8x13-0

L L

Living
13-5x13-0

Porch depth 4-0

PLAN NUMBER: 586-007D-0062

PRICE CODE: D

PLAN DETAILS

- 2,483 total square feet of living area
- A large entry porch with open brick arches and palladian door welcomes guests
- The vaulted great room features an entertainment center alcove and the ideal layout for furniture placement
- The dining room is extra large with a stylish tray ceiling
- A convenient kitchen with wrap-around counter, menu desk and pantry opens to the cozy breakfast area
- 4 bedrooms, 2 baths, 2-car side entry garage
- Basement foundation

Rear View

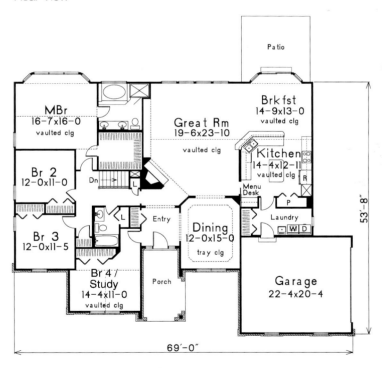

Patio

Brk fst
14-9x13-0
vaulted clg

MBr
16-7x16-0
vaulted clg

Great Rm
19-6x23-10

vaulted clg

Kitchen
14-4x12-11
vaulted clg

Br 2
12-0x11-0

Dn

L

Menu
Desk

P

R

Entry

Dining
12-0x15-0

Laundry

Br 3
12-0x11-5

L

W D

tray clg

Br 4 /
Study
14-4x11-0

Porch

Garage
22-4x20-4

vaulted clg

53'-8"

69'-0"

PLAN DETAILS

- 1,674 total square feet of living area
- Vaulted great room, dining area and kitchen all enjoy a central fireplace and log bin
- Convenient laundry/mud room is located between the garage and the rest of the home with handy stairs to the basement
- Easily expandable screened porch and adjacent patio access the dining area
- 3 bedrooms, 2 baths, 2-car garage
- Basement foundation, drawings also include crawl space and slab foundations

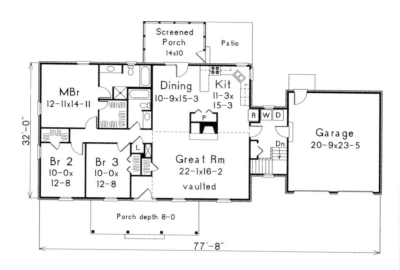

Screened
Porch
14x10

Patio

MBr
12-11x14-11

Dining
10-9x15-3

Kit
11-3x
15-3

32'-0"

R W D

Garage
20-9x23-5

P

Br 2
10-0x
12-8

Br 3
10-0x
12-8

L

Great Rm
22-1x16-2

vaulted

Dn

Porch depth 8-0

77'-8"

Rear View

PLAN DETAILS

- 1,945 total square feet of living area
- Master suite is separate from other bedrooms for privacy
- Vaulted breakfast room is directly off the great room
- Kitchen includes a built-in desk area
- Elegant dining room has an arched window
- 4 bedrooms, 2 baths, 2-car side entry garage
- Walk-out basement, crawl space or slab foundation, please specify when ordering

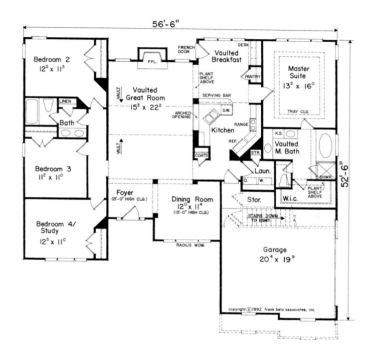

56'-6"

52'-6"

Bedroom 2
12⁵ x 11³

FPL.

FRENCH DOOR

DESK

Vaulted Breakfast

Master Suite
13² x 16⁰

VAULT

Vaulted Great Room
15³ x 22²

PLANT SHELF ABOVE

PANTRY

TRAY CLG.

LINEN

SERVING BAR

Bath

ARCHED OPENING

D.W.

RANGE

Kitchen

K.S.

Vaulted M. Bath

VAULT

REF.

Bedroom 3
11² x 11⁰

COATS

STR.

Laun.

T. SHWR.

PLANT SHELF ABOVE

Foyer
(13'-0" HIGH CLG.)

D.

W.

W.i.c.

Dining Room
12⁰ x 11⁴
(13'-0" HIGH CLG.)

Stor.

Bedroom 4/
Study
12⁵ x 11⁰

STAIRS DOWN TO BSMT.

RADIUS WDW.

Garage
20⁴ x 19⁹

copyright Ⓒ 1992 frank betz associates, inc.

PLAN NUMBER: 586-007D-0001
PRICE CODE: E

PLAN DETAILS

- 2,597 total square feet of living area
- Large U-shaped kitchen features an island cooktop and breakfast bar
- Entry and great room are enhanced by sweeping balcony
- Bedrooms #2 and #3 share a bath, while bedroom #4 has a private bath
- Vaulted great room includes transomed arch windows
- 4 bedrooms, 3 1/2 baths, 2-car side entry garage
- Walk-out basement foundation, drawings also include crawl space and slab foundations

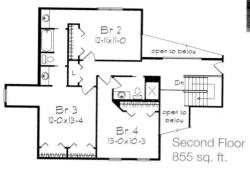

Br 2
12-11x11-0

open to below

Br 3
12-0x13-4

Dn

open to below

Br 4
13-0x10-3

Second Floor
855 sq. ft.

61'-4"

Screened
Porch

Deck

vaulted

Great Rm
17-0x17-0

Hearth Rm
15-8x13-0

Kitchen

vaulted

14-0x13-0

48'-0"

Dn

Up

Dining
12-0x15-9

Entry

MBr
18-4x17-5

vaulted

Garage
21-4x21-4

First Floor
1,742 sq. ft.

PLAN DETAILS

- 1,992 total square feet of living area
- Bayed breakfast room overlooks the outdoor deck and connects to the screened porch
- Private formal living room in the front of the home could easily be converted to a home office or study
- Compact, yet efficient kitchen is conveniently situated between the breakfast and dining rooms
- 3 bedrooms, 2 1/2 baths, 3-car side entry garage
- Basement, crawl space or slab foundation, please specify when ordering

Rear View

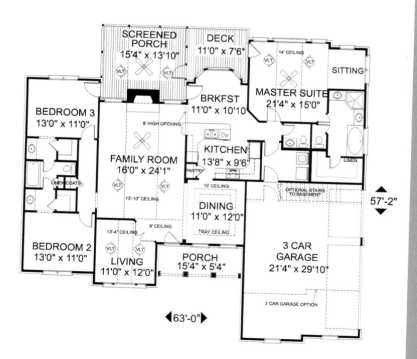

SCREENED PORCH
15'4" x 13'10"

DECK
11'0" x 7'6"

14' CEILING

SITTING

MASTER SUITE
21'4" x 15'0"

BEDROOM 3
13'0" x 11'0"

BRKFST
11'0" x 10'10

8' HIGH OPENING

KITCHEN
13'8" x 9'6"

DW

FAMILY ROOM
16'0" x 24'1"

PANTRY

LINEN COATS

13'-10" CEILING

10' CEILING

LINEN

OPTIONAL STAIRS TO BASEMENT

57'-2"

DINING
11'0" x 12'0"

TRAY CEILING

13'-4" CEILING

9' CEILING

BEDROOM 2
13'0" x 11'0"

LIVING
11'0" x 12'0"

PORCH
15'4" x 5'4"

3 CAR GARAGE
21'4" x 29'10"

2 CAR GARAGE OPTION

◀63'-0"▶

PLAN DETAILS

- 1,477 total square feet of living area
- Oversized porch provides protection from the elements
- Innovative kitchen employs step-saving design
- Kitchen has snack bar which opens to the breakfast room with bay window
- 3 bedrooms, 2 baths, 2-car side entry garage with storage area
- Basement foundation

Rear View

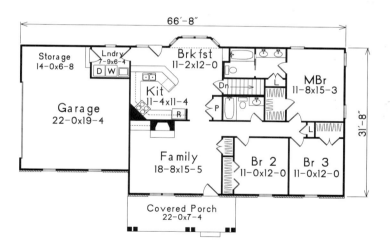

66'-8"

Storage
14-0x6-8

Lndry
7-9x6-4

D W

Brkfst
11-2x12-0

Kit
11-4x11-4

Garage
22-0x19-4

R

Dn

P

MBr
11-8x15-3

L

L

31'-8"

Family
18-8x15-5

Br 2
11-0x12-0

Br 3
11-0x12-0

Covered Porch
22-0x7-4

99

PLAN DETAILS

- 2,218 total square feet of living area
- Vaulted great room has an arched colonnade entry, bay windowed atrium with staircase and a fireplace
- Vaulted kitchen enjoys bay doors to deck, pass-through breakfast bar and walk-in pantry
- Breakfast room offers a bay window and snack bar open to the kitchen with a large laundry room nearby
- Atrium opens to 1,217 square feet of optional living area below
- 4 bedrooms, 2 baths, 2-car garage
- Walk-out basement foundation

Rear View

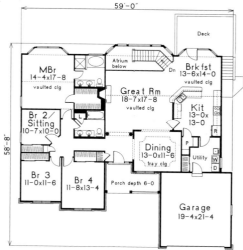

First Floor
2,218 sq. ft.

59'-0"

58'-8"

Deck

MBr
14-4x17-8
vaulted clg

Atrium
below

Brkfst
13-6x14-0
vaulted clg

Dn

Great Rm
18-7x17-8
vaulted clg

Kit
13-0x
13-0

Br 2/
Sitting
10-7x10-0

Dining
13-0x11-6
tray clg

P

Utility

R

W
D

Br 3
11-0x11-6

Br 4
11-8x13-4

Porch depth 6-0

Garage
19-4x21-4

Optional
Lower Level
1,217 sq. ft.

Up

Atrium

Br 6
14-9x15-2

Family Rm
18-7x24-5

Br 5
12-4x15-2

Up

Wet
Bar

F

Unfinished Area

PLAN DETAILS

- 1,404 total square feet of living area
- Split-foyer entrance
- Bayed living area features a unique vaulted ceiling and fireplace
- Wrap-around kitchen has corner windows for added sunlight and a bar that overlooks dining area
- Master bath features a garden tub with separate shower
- Rear deck provides handy access to the dining room and kitchen
- 3 bedrooms, 2 baths, 2-car drive under garage
- Basement foundation, drawings also include partial crawl space foundation

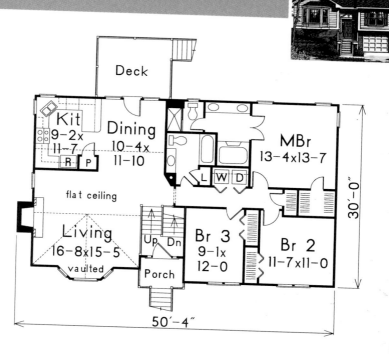

Deck

Kit
9-2x
11-7

Dining
10-4x
11-10

R P

MBr
13-4x13-7

flat ceiling

L W D

Living
16-8x15-5
vaulted

Up Dn

Br 3
9-1x
12-0

Br 2
11-7x11-0

Porch

30'-0"

50'-4"

Rear View

PLAN NUMBER: 586-021D-0007

PRICE CODE: D

PLAN DETAILS

- 1,868 total square feet of living area
- Luxurious master bath is impressive with an angled quarter-circle tub, separate vanities and large walk-in closet
- Energy efficient home with 2" x 6" exterior walls
- Dining room is surrounded by a series of arched openings which complement the open feeling of this design
- Living room has a 12' ceiling accented by skylights and a large fireplace flanked by sliding doors
- 3 bedrooms, 2 baths, 2-car side entry garage
- Slab foundation, drawings also include crawl space foundation

Rear View

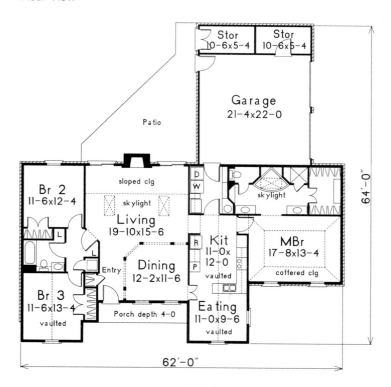

Stor
10-6x5-4

Stor
10-6x5-4

Garage
21-4x22-0

Patio

sloped clg

Br 2
11-6x12-4

skylight

D
W

skylight

Living
19-10x15-6

L

Entry

L

Dining
12-2x11-6

R
P

Kit
11-0x
12-0
vaulted

MBr
17-8x13-4

coffered clg

Br 3
11-6x13-4
vaulted

Porch depth 4-0

Eating
11-0x9-6
vaulted

64'-0"

62'-0"

PLAN DETAILS

- 2,695 total square feet of living area
- A grand-scale great room features a fireplace with flanking shelves, handsome entry foyer with staircase and opens to a large kitchen and breakfast room
- Roomy master bedroom has a bay window, huge walk-in closet and bath with a shower built for two
- Bedrooms #2 and #3 are generously oversized with walk-in closets and a Jack and Jill style bath
- 3 bedrooms, 2 1/2 baths, 2-car side entry garage
- Basement foundation

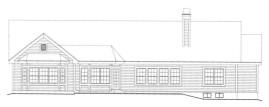

Rear View

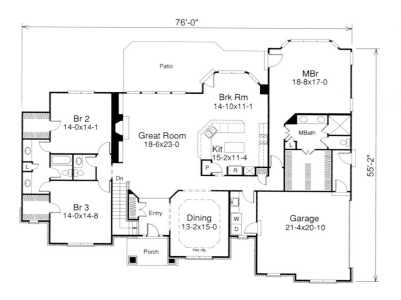

76'-0"

Patio

MBr
18-8x17-0

Br 2
14-0x14-1

Brk Rm
14-10x11-1

Great Room
18-6x23-0

MBath

Kit
15-2x11-4

L

P   R

Dn

Br 3
14-0x14-8

Entry

Dining
13-2x15-0

tray clg.

Garage
21-4x20-10

W
D

Porch

55'-2"

PLAN DETAILS

- 1,704 total square feet of living area
- Open floor plan combines foyer, dining and living rooms together for an open airy feeling
- Kitchen has island that adds workspace and storage
- Bedrooms are situated together and secluded from the rest of the home
- 3 bedrooms, 2 baths
- Slab foundation

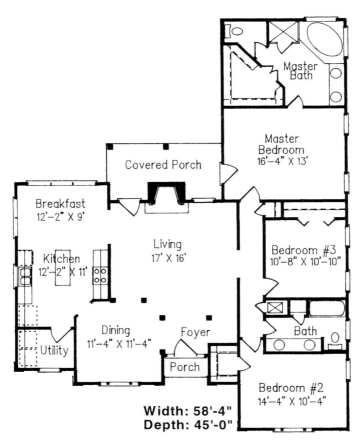

Master
Bath

Master
Bedroom
16'-4" X 13'

Covered Porch

Breakfast
12'-2" X 9'

Living
17' X 16'

Bedroom #3
10'-8" X 10'-10"

Kitchen
12'-2" X 11'

Dining
11'-4" X 11'-4"

Foyer

Bath

Utility

Porch

Bedroom #2
14'-4" X 10'-4"

Width: 58'-4"
Depth: 45'-0"

PLAN DETAILS

- 1,842 total square feet of living area
- Vaulted family room features a fireplace and an elegant bookcase
- Island countertop in kitchen makes cooking convenient
- Rear facade has an intimate porch area ideal for relaxing
- 3 bedrooms, 2 baths, 2-car garage
- Slab or crawl space foundation, please specify when ordering

Width: 56'-4"
Depth: 68'-6"

Porch
11 x 6/10

Family Room
14 x 17/1

12' Vaulted Clg.

Breakfast
10/9 x 11/6

9' Ceiling

Bookcase

Master
14 x 16

9' Ceiling

Skylight

Kitchen
17/5 x 9

P

Br. #2
11 x 12/10

9' Ceiling

L

Skylight

Foyer
6 x 8

Dining
11 x12

10' Ceiling

Utility
W D

Br. #3
11 x12

9' Ceiling

L

Porch

Garage
22 x 22

PLAN DETAILS

- 1,684 total square feet of living area
- Wrap-around porch is anchored by a full masonry fireplace
- The vaulted great room includes a large bay window, fireplace, dining balcony and atrium window wall
- Double walk-in closets, large luxury bath and sliding doors to an exterior balcony are a few fantastic features of the master bedroom
- Atrium opens to 611 square feet of optional living area on the lower level
- 3 bedrooms, 2 baths, 2-car drive under garage
- Walk-out basement foundation

55'-8"

46'-4"

Balcony

MBr
18-4x13-0

Kit
10-2x
11-9

Dining   Dn

Great Rm
16-0x21-4
vaulted

W D

Entry

Porch depth 6-0

Br 2
12-8x14-0

Br 3
11-4x12-6

First Floor
1,684 sq. ft.

Up

Garage
22-4x26-8

Family
15-6x20-8

Unfinished

Optional
Lower Level
611 sq. ft.

Rear View

PLAN NUMBER: 586-040D-0011

PRICE CODE: B

PLAN DETAILS

- 1,739 total square feet of living area
- Utility room has convenient laundry sink
- Vaulted ceiling lends drama to the family room with fireplace and double French doors
- Island kitchen is enhanced by adjoining breakfast area with access to the patio
- Formal dining room features a 10' ceiling
- Private hallway separates the bedrooms from the living area
- 3 bedrooms, 2 baths, 2-car side entry garage
- Slab foundation

114

Rear View

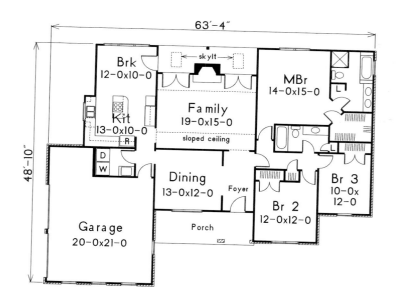

63'-4"

48'-10"

Brk
12-0x10-0

skylt

MBr
14-0x15-0

Kit
13-0x10-0

Family
19-0x15-0

sloped ceiling

D
W

Dining
13-0x12-0

Foyer

Br 3
10-0x
12-0

Garage
20-0x21-0

Porch

Br 2
12-0x12-0

PLAN DETAILS

- 1,565 total square feet of living area
- Centrally located master bedroom
- Vaulted ceilings throughout this home
- Well-organized kitchen with convenient pantry and utility closets
- 3 bedrooms, 2 baths, 2-car garage
- Slab foundation

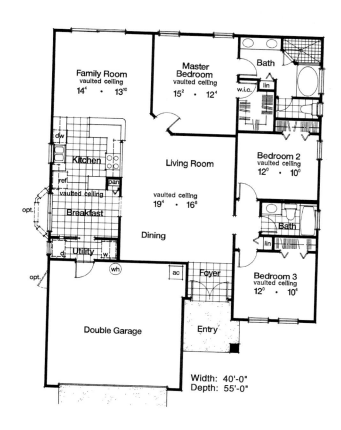

Family Room
vaulted ceiling
14⁴ · 13¹⁰

Master Bedroom
vaulted ceiling
15² · 12⁴

Bath

w.i.c. lin

dw

Kitchen

ref.

vaulted ceiling

pan

opt.

Breakfast

Living Room

vaulted ceiling
19⁴ · 16⁸

Bedroom 2
vaulted ceiling
12⁰ · 10⁰

Bath

lin

Dining

d. **Utility** w.

wh

ac

Foyer

opt.

Double Garage

Entry

Bedroom 3
vaulted ceiling
12⁰ · 10⁴

Width: 40'-0"
Depth: 55'-0"

PLAN DETAILS

- 1,991 total square feet of living area
- A large porch with roof dormers and flanking stonework creates a distinctive country appeal
- The highly functional U-shaped kitchen is open to the dining and living rooms defined by a colonnade
- Large bay windows are enjoyed by both the living room and master bedroom
- Each bedroom has a walk-in closet and their own private bath
- 3 bedrooms, 3 1/2 baths, 2-car side entry garage
- Basement foundation

Patio

MBr
17-0x12-8

Living
21-0x16-6

Br 2
11-8x14-6

Dn

Garage
21-4x23-3

38'-4"

W
D

L P
R

Kit
10-0 x
10-9

Brk fst
10-0x11-10

Entry

Br 3
15-8x12-6

Porch depth 6-0

85'-6"

Rear View

PLAN DETAILS

- 1,787 total square feet of living area
- Private master bedroom features an enormous tub, walk-in closet and close proximity to the laundry room
- A Jack and Jill style bath is shared by bedrooms #2 and #3
- 12' ceiling in foyer makes a dramatic entrance
- 3 bedrooms, 2 1/2 baths, 2-car garage
- Walk-out basement foundation

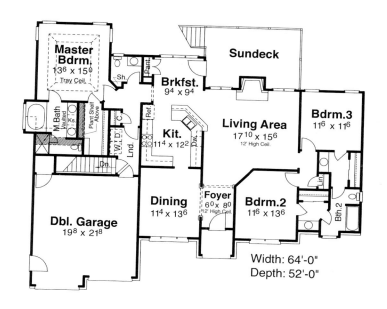

Master Bdrm.
13⁶ x 15⁰
Tray Ceil.

Sh.

Pant.

Sundeck

Brkfst.
9⁴ x 9⁴

Bdrm.3
11⁶ x 11⁶

M.Bath
Vaulted

Ks

Plant Shelf Above

W.D.

C.

Ref.

Kit.
11⁴ x 12²

Living Area
17¹⁰ x 15⁶
12' High Ceil.

Lnd.

Dw.

Dn.

Dining
11⁴ x 13⁶

Foyer
6⁰ x 8⁰
12' High Ceil.

Bdrm.2
11⁶ x 13⁶

Bth.2

Dbl. Garage
19⁸ x 21⁸

Width: 64'-0"
Depth: 52'-0"

PLAN DETAILS

- 2,328 total square feet of living area
- Formal living and dining rooms feature floor-to-ceiling windows
- Kitchen with island counter and pantry makes cooking a delight
- Expansive master bedroom has luxury bath with double vanity and walk-in closet
- 4 bedrooms, 2 1/2 baths, 2-car garage
- Basement foundation, drawings also include slab and crawl space foundations

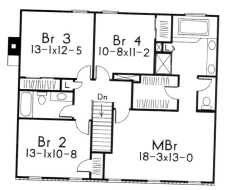

Br 3
13-1x12-5

Br 4
10-8x11-2

Dn

Br 2
13-1x10-8

MBr
18-3x13-0

Second Floor
1,140 sq. ft.

Patio

First Floor
1,188 sq. ft.

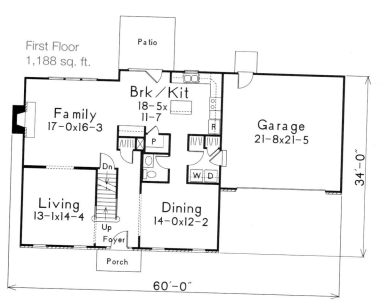

Family
17-0x16-3

Brk/Kit
18-5x
11-7

Garage
21-8x21-5

Dn

Living
13-1x14-4

Up
Foyer

Dining
14-0x12-2

W D

R

P

Porch

34'-0"

60'-0"

PLAN DETAILS

- 2,058 total square feet of living area
- Handsome two-story foyer with balcony creates a spacious entrance area
- Master bedroom has a private dressing area and walk-in closet
- Skylights furnish natural lighting in the hall and master bath
- Laundry closet is conveniently located on the second floor near the bedrooms
- 3 bedrooms, 2 1/2 baths, 2-car garage
- Basement foundation, drawings also include slab and crawl space foundations

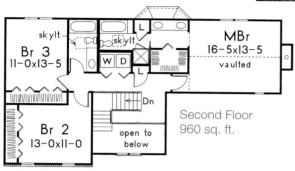

Br 3
11-0x13-5

skylt

skylt

L

W D

L

MBr
16-5x13-5

vaulted

Dn

Br 2
13-0x11-0

open to
below

Second Floor
960 sq. ft.

First Floor
1,098 sq. ft.

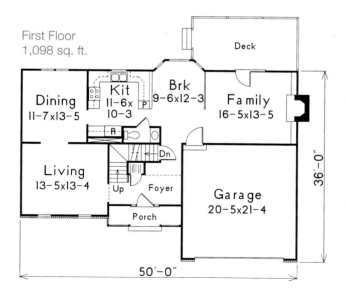

Deck

Dining
11-7x13-5

Kit
11-6x
10-3

Brk
9-6x12-3

Family
16-5x13-5

R

Living
13-5x13-4

Dn

Up

Foyer

Garage
20-5x21-4

Porch

36'-0"

50'-0"

PLAN NUMBER: 586-055D-0193

PRICE CODE: D

PLAN DETAILS

- 2,131 total square feet of living area
- The kitchen, great room and dining room create an expansive living area
- Bedroom #2 features a charming bay window with seat
- The garage includes space for a safe storm shelter
- 3 bedrooms, 2 1/2 baths, 2-car side entry garage
- Slab or crawl space foundation, please specify when ordering

63'-10"

GAS
BIBB

GRILLING
PATIO
13'-4" X 12'-0"

SCREENED
PORCH
29'-8" X 12'-0"

MASTER
SUITE
13'-0" X 17'-2"

GREAT RM.
18'-0" X 22'-0"

DINING
13'-8" X 13'-8"

M.BATH
15'-0" X 17'-4"

VAULTED
CEILING

SKYLIGHTS

LIN

MC

VAULTED
CEILING

RANGE
W/ MW

BATH

MC LIN

COMPUTER
CENTER

DW

KITCHEN
12'-10" X 10'-6"

REF

FRENCH
DOORS

PANTRY

W

LAU.
8'-7" X 7'-8"

KID'S
NOOK
BENCH /
HANGING

72'-2"

WINDOW
SEAT

BEDROOM 2
14'-8" X 12'-6"

BEDROOM 3 /
DEN
13'-6" X 14'-2"

FOYER
7'-7" X 11'-10"

STORM
SHELTER

D

DN

COVERED PORCH
36'-8" X 8'-0"

OPTIONAL BASEMENT PLAN

GARAGE
21'-0" X 27'-4"

PLAN DETAILS

- 1,340 total square feet of living area
- Grand-sized vaulted living and dining rooms offer fireplace, wet bar and breakfast counter open to spacious kitchen
- Vaulted master bedroom features a double-door entry, walk-in closet and an elegant bath
- Basement includes a huge two-car garage and space for a bedroom/bath expansion
- 3 bedrooms, 2 baths, 2-car drive under garage with storage area
- Basement foundation

Rear View

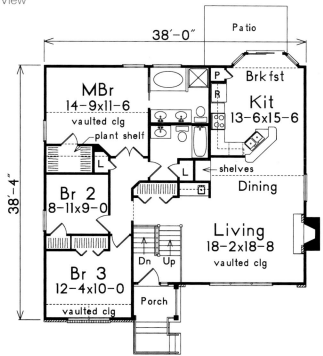

38'-0"

Patio

MBr
14-9x11-6
vaulted clg

plant shelf

L

Br 2
8-11x9-0

Br 3
12-4x10-0

vaulted clg

Dn Up

Porch

P
R

Brkfst

Kit
13-6x15-6

shelves

L

Dining

Living
18-2x18-8
vaulted clg

38'-4"

PLAN DETAILS

- 1,770 total square feet of living area
- 12' ceilings enhance the living and dining rooms, kitchen, breakfast nook and foyer
- The secluded master bedroom enjoys a private bath with a walk-in closet and double-bowl vanity
- The kitchen opens to the living and dining rooms for an easy flow of family activities
- 3 bedrooms, 2 baths, 2-car side entry garage
- Slab foundation, drawings also include crawl space foundation

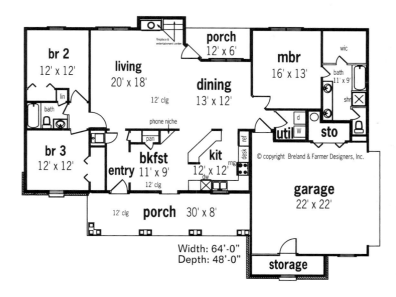

br 2
12' x 12'

living
20' x 18'
12' clg

lin

bath

br 3
12' x 12'

entry

phone niche

pan

bkfst
11' x 9'
12' clg

fireplace &
entertainment center

porch
12' x 6'

dining
13' x 12'

kit
12' x 12'
dw

rng

desk

ref

mbr
16' x 13'

wic

bath
11' x 9'

shr

d

w

util

sto

© copyright Breland & Farmer Designers, Inc.

garage
22' x 22'

12' clg

porch 30' x 8'

Width: 64'-0"
Depth: 48'-0"

storage

PLAN DETAILS

- 1,849 total square feet of living area
- Open floor plan creates an airy feeling
- Kitchen and breakfast area include center island, pantry and built-in desk
- Master bedroom has a private entrance off the breakfast area and a view of the vaulted porch
- 3 bedrooms, 2 baths, 2-car garage
- Crawl space or slab foundation, please specify when ordering

Width: 66'-5"
Depth: 60'-0"

Porch
12/4 x 14/3

Vaulted Ceiling

Master
18 x 14

Recessed Ceiling

Breakfast
12/4 x 10/8

Desk

9' Ceiling

Br. #2
12 x 11

9' Ceiling

Family Room
20 x 15/3

11'-7" Ceiling

Kitchen
14/4 x 9/8

Utility
9/8 x 8/10

L

P

W D

Foyer
8/8 x 11/7

Dining
13/4 x 11/7

11'-7" Ceiling

Garage
24 x 24

Br. #3
12 x 11

9' Ceiling

Porch
11/4 x 6

PLAN DETAILS

- 2,286 total square feet of living area
- Fine architectural detail makes this home a showplace with its large windows, intricate brickwork and fine woodwork and trim
- Two-story entry with attractive wood railing and balustrades in foyer
- Convenient wrap-around kitchen enjoys a window view, planning center and pantry
- Master bedroom includes a walk-in closet and master bath
- 4 bedrooms, 2 1/2 baths, 2-car garage
- Basement foundation, drawings also include crawl space and slab foundations

Br 4
10-2x
10-8

Br 3
11-7x10-8

MBr
12-8x15-11
vaulted

Dn

Br 2
12-4x10-8

open to
below

Second Floor
1,003 sq. ft.

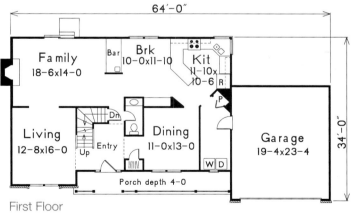

64'-0"

Family
18-6x14-0

Bar

Brk
10-0x11-10

Kit
11-10x
10-6

R

P

Living
12-8x16-0

Dn

Up

Entry

Dining
11-0x13-0

Garage
19-4x23-4

34'-0"

W D

Porch depth 4-0

First Floor
1,283 sq. ft.

135

PLAN DETAILS

- 2,024 total square feet of living area
- Impressive fireplace and sloped ceiling in the family room
- Master bedroom features a vaulted ceiling, separate dressing room and a walk-in closet
- Breakfast area includes a work desk and accesses the deck
- 4 bedrooms, 2 1/2 baths, 2-car side entry garage
- Basement foundation

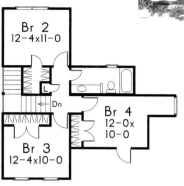

Second Floor
629 sq. ft.

Br 2
12-4x11-0

Dn
L

Br 4
12-0x
10-0

Br 3
12-4x10-0

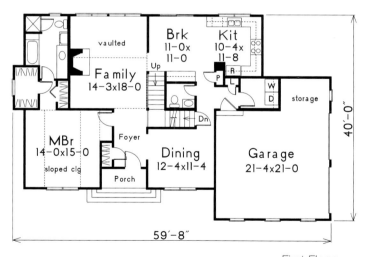

vaulted

Brk
11-0x
11-0

Kit
10-4x
11-8

Up

Family
14-3x18-0

P
R
L

W
D

storage

Dn

MBr
14-0x15-0

Foyer

Dining
12-4x11-4

Garage
21-4x21-0

sloped clg

Porch

40'-0"

59'-8"

First Floor
1,395 sq. ft.

137

PLAN DETAILS

- 2,408 total square feet of living area
- Large vaulted great room overlooks atrium and window wall, adjoins dining room, spacious breakfast room with bay and pass-through kitchen
- A special private bedroom with bath, separate from other bedrooms, is perfect for mother-in-law suite or children home from college
- Atrium opens to 1,100 square feet of optional living area below
- 4 bedrooms, 3 baths, 3-car side entry garage
- Walk-out basement foundation

First Floor
2,408 sq. ft.

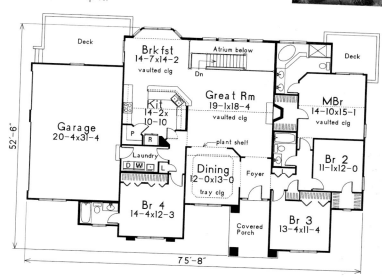

Deck

Brk fst
14-7x14-2
vaulted clg

Atrium below

Dn

Deck

Garage
20-4x31-4

Kit
14-2x
10-10

P

R

Great Rm
19-1x18-4
vaulted clg

MBr
14-10x15-1
vaulted clg

plant shelf

Laundry

D W L

Dining
12-0x13-0
tray clg

Br 4
14-4x12-3

Foyer

Br 2
11-1x12-0

Covered
Porch

Br 3
13-4x11-4

52'-6"

75'-8"

Optional
Lower Level
1,100 sq. ft.

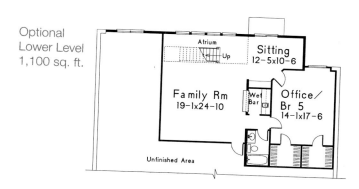

Atrium

Up

Sitting
12-5x10-6

Family Rm
19-1x24-10

Wet
Bar

**Office/
Br 5**
14-1x17-6

Unfinished Area

PLAN DETAILS

- 1,768 total square feet of living area
- Uniquely designed vaulted living and dining rooms combine making great use of space
- Informal family room has a vaulted ceiling, plant shelf accents and kitchen overlook
- Sunny breakfast area conveniently accesses kitchen
- 3 bedrooms, 2 baths, 2-car garage
- Slab foundation

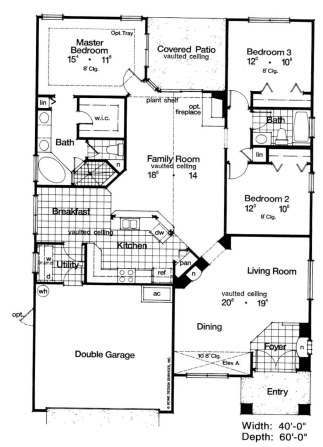

Opt. Tray

Master Bedroom
15⁴ • 11⁸
8' Clg.

Covered Patio
vaulted ceiling

Bedroom 3
12⁰ • 10⁸
8' Clg.

lin

plant shelf

opt. fireplace

w.i.c.

Bath

Bath

lin

Family Room
vaulted ceiling
18⁸ • 14

n

Breakfast

Bedroom 2
12⁰ • 10⁸
8' Clg.

vaulted ceiling

Kitchen

dw

pan

w

Utility

d

ref

n

Living Room

vaulted ceiling
20⁸ • 19⁴

wh

ac

opt.

Dining

Double Garage

10' 8" Clg.

Elev. A.

Foyer

n

© HOME DESIGN SERVICES, INC.

Entry

Width: 40'-0"
Depth: 60'-0"

PLAN DETAILS

- 1,381 total square feet of living area
- Plenty of closet space in all the bedrooms
- Kitchen has a large eating bar for extra dining
- Great room has a sunny wall of windows creating a cheerful atmosphere
- 3 bedrooms, 2 baths, 2-car garage
- Slab, crawl space, walk-out basement or basement foundation, please specify when ordering

48' 0"

48' 0"

MASTER SUITE
13'-6" X 13'-6"

9' BOXED CEILING

GREAT ROOM
17'-0" X 13'-6"

GAS FIREPLACE

9' BOXED CEILING

BEDROOM 3
11'-4" X 11'-8"

LIN

BATH

DW

REF

KITCHEN

BATH

W

RG

D

DINING
11'-2" X 13'-8"

FOYER

HVAC

STRG.

WH

PRCH

BEDROOM 2
11'-4" X 11'-6"

VAULTED CEILING

GARAGE
19'-4" X 21'-6"

PLAN DETAILS

- 1,865 total square feet of living area
- The large foyer opens into an expansive dining area and great room
- Home features vaulted ceilings throughout
- Master bedroom features an angled entry, vaulted ceiling, plant shelf and bath with double vanity, tub and shower
- 4 bedrooms, 2 baths, 2-car garage
- Slab foundation, drawings also include crawl space foundation

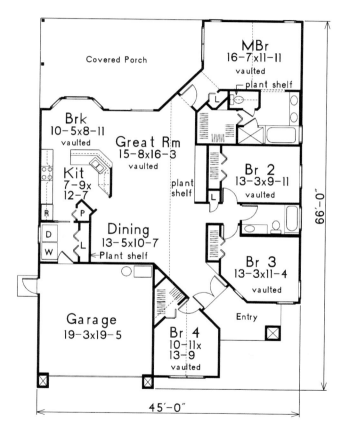

Covered Porch

MBr
16-7x11-11
vaulted

plant shelf

L

Brk
10-5x8-11
vaulted

Great Rm
15-8x16-3
vaulted

Kit
7-9x
12-7

plant
shelf

Br 2
13-3x9-11
vaulted

L

R

P

D

L

Dining
13-5x10-7
←Plant shelf

W

Br 3
13-3x11-4
vaulted

Garage
19-3x19-5

Br 4
10-11x
13-9
vaulted

Entry

66'-0"

45'-0"

145

PLAN DETAILS

- 2,405 total square feet of living area
- Grilling porch and covered porch combine for an outdoor living area
- The master suite enjoys a bayed sitting area and luxurious bath with large walk-in closet
- Kitchen, breakfast and hearth rooms combine for a family living area
- Optional second floor has an additional 358 square feet of living space
- 4 bedrooms, 3 baths, 3-car side entry garage
- Slab or crawl space foundation, please specify when ordering

66'-4"

67'-2"

BREAKFAST ROOM
11'-0" X 9'-0"

GRILLING PORCH
10'-4" X 7'-8"

COVERED PORCH
18'-0" X 11'-8"

WHP TUB

GLASS SHWR

SITTING ROOM
9'-4" X 9'-4"

GAS FIREPLACE

HEARTH ROOM
11'-0" X 14'-0"

DW

C.T.

FRENCH DOORS

MEDIA CENTER

M.BATH
11'-8" X 22'-0"

LIN

MASTER SUITE
13'-6" X 15'-3"

COMPUTER CENTER

KITCHEN
10'-4" X 15'-0"

OVEN

REF

GREAT ROOM
10' CEILING
18'-0" X 17'-4"

BEDROOM 4
11'-4" X 10'-8"

LAU.
8'-4" X 6'-6"

PANTRY

UP

8" COLUMNS

DINING ROOM
10' CEILING
11'-0" X 12'-6"

FOYER
10' CEILING
7'-0" X 12'-6"

LIN

BEDROOM 3
11'-4" X 10'-11"

GARAGE
21'-4" X 34'-4"

PORCH
18'-0" X 5'-0"

8" COLUMNS

OPT. DOOR

BEDROOM 2/ STUDY
11' CEILING
14'-0" X 12'-0"

BOOK SHELVES

BATH

© 2001 NELSON DESIGN GROUP, LLC.

First Floor
2,405 sq. ft.

DN

BONUS ROOM
11'-8" X 29'-0"

5'-8" LINE

6'-8" LINE

5' WALLS

5' WALLS

Optional Second Floor
358 sq. ft.

PLAN DETAILS

- 2,215 total square feet of living area
- Two-story living room is open to the dining room and combined breakfast area and kitchen for an open feel
- Master bedroom has a window seat and includes a bath with large tub, double vanity and separate shower
- Laundry room is located on the second floor for added convenience
- 4 bedrooms, 3 baths, 2-car side entry garage
- Walk-out basement foundation

Second Floor
1,140 sq. ft.

Bdrm.3
11^0 x 11^0

Opt. Plant Shelf Above

Open To Living Area

Opt. Vault

Laund.

W. D.

Sh. | Seat
Stepped Tray | Sh.

Master Bdrm.
13^6 x 17^6

Computer Station

Bath 2

Dn.

Opt. Plant Shelf Above

Open To Foyer

Bdrm.2
10^8 x 11^0

Opt. Vault

Plant Shelf Above

M.Bath
Tray

Low Storage

M.Clos.

Low Storage

First Floor
1,075 sq. ft.

Patio / Sundeck

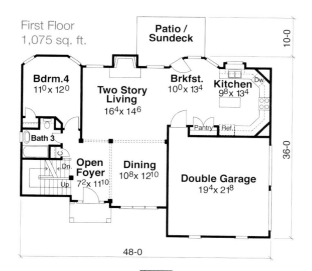

Bdrm.4
11^0 x 12^0

Two Story Living
16^4 x 14^6

Brkfst.
10^0 x 13^4

Kitchen
9^8 x 13^4

Dw

10-0

Bath 3

Pantry | Ref.

Open Foyer
7^2 x 11^{10}

Dn.
Up

Dining
10^8 x 12^{10}

Double Garage
19^4 x 21^8

36-0

48-0

PLAN DETAILS

- 1,591 total square feet of living area
- Spacious porch and patio provide outdoor enjoyment
- Large entry foyer leads to a cheery kitchen and breakfast room which welcomes the sun through a wide array of windows
- The great room features a vaulted ceiling, corner fireplace, wet bar and access to the rear patio
- Double walk-in closets, private porch and a luxury bath are special highlights of the vaulted master bedroom suite
- 3 bedrooms, 2 baths, 2-car side entry garage
- Basement foundation

Rear View

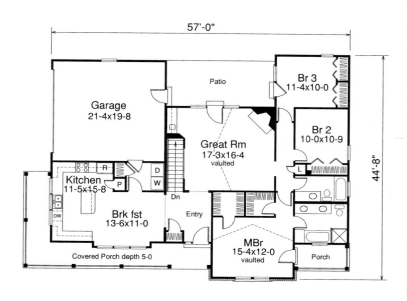

57'-0"

Garage
21-4x19-8

Patio

Br 3
11-4x10-0

Br 2
10-0x10-9

Great Rm
17-3x16-4
vaulted

Kitchen
11-5x15-8

R

D
W

Dn

P

L

Brk fst
13-6x11-0

Entry

DW

MBr
15-4x12-0
vaulted

Porch

44'-8"

Covered Porch depth 5-0

151

PLAN DETAILS

- 1,609 total square feet of living area
- Efficient kitchen includes a corner pantry and adjacent laundry room
- Breakfast room boasts plenty of windows and opens onto rear deck
- Master bedroom features a tray ceiling and private deluxe bath
- Entry opens into large living area with fireplace
- 4 bedrooms, 2 baths, 2-car garage
- Basement foundation

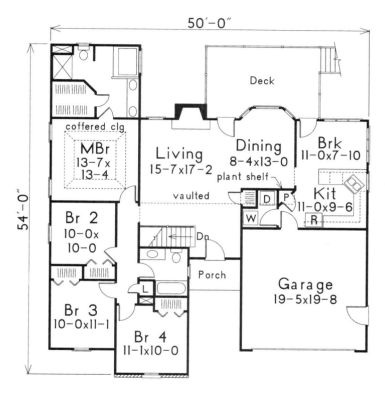

50'-0"

54'-0"

Deck

coffered clg

MBr
13-7x
13-4

Living
15-7x17-2

Dining
8-4x13-0

Brk
11-0x7-10

plant shelf

vaulted

Kit
11-0x9-6

D P

W

R

Br 2
10-0x
10-0

Dn

Porch

Garage
19-5x19-8

Br 3
10-0x11-1

L

Br 4
11-1x10-0

PLAN DETAILS

- 1,538 total square feet of living area
- Dining and great rooms are highlighted in this design
- Master suite has many amenities
- Kitchen and laundry room are accessible from any room in the house
- 3 bedrooms, 2 baths, 2-car garage
- Walk-out basement, basement, crawl space or slab foundation, please specify when ordering

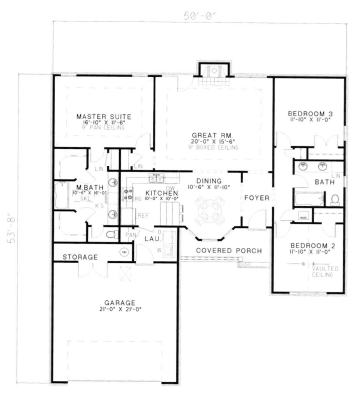

50'-0"

53'-8"

MASTER SUITE
16'-10" X 11'-6"
9' PAN CEILING

GREAT RM.
20'-0" X 15'-6"
9' BOXED CEILING

BEDROOM 3
11'-10" X 11'-0"

LIN

LIN

DINING
10'-6" X 11'-10"

BATH

M.BATH
10'-6" X 16'-0"
SKL

KITCHEN
10'-0" X 10'-0"

FOYER

K S

RG

DW

REF

HVAC

PAN

D

LAU.

W

COVERED PORCH

BEDROOM 2
11'-10" X 11'-0"

STORAGE

WH

VAULTED
CEILING

GARAGE
21'-0" X 21'-0"

PLAN DETAILS

- 1,741 total square feet of living area
- Handsome exterior has multiple gables and elegant brickwork
- The great room offers a fireplace, vaulted ceiling and is open to the bayed dining area and kitchen with breakfast bar
- The master bedroom boasts a vaulted ceiling, large walk-in closet, luxury bath and enjoys a nearby room perfect for a study, nursery or fifth bedroom
- 4 bedrooms, 2 baths, 2-car garage
- Crawl space foundation, drawings also inclue slab and basement foundations

Rear View

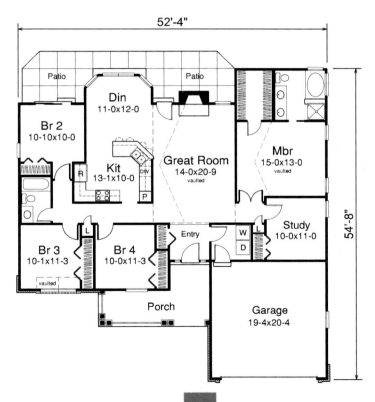

52'-4"

54'-8"

Patio

Patio

Din
11-0x12-0

Br 2
10-10x10-0

Kit
13-1x10-0

DW

R

P

Great Room
14-0x20-9
vaulted

Mbr
15-0x13-0
vaulted

Br 3
10-1x11-3

L

Br 4
10-0x11-3

Entry

W
D

L

Study
10-0x11-0

vaulted

Porch

Garage
19-4x20-4

PLAN DETAILS

- 1,865 total square feet of living area
- The family room, breakfast area and kitchen combine forming a large open area for family activities
- A double-door entry leads to the grand master bedroom which includes two walk-in closets and a private bath
- Bedrooms #2 and #3 enjoy walk-in closets and share a bath
- 3 bedrooms, 2 1/2 baths, 2-car garage
- Basement foundation

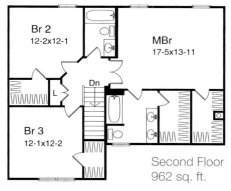

Br 2
12-2x12-1

MBr
17-5x13-11

Dn

L

Br 3
12-1x12-2

Second Floor
962 sq. ft.

38'-0"

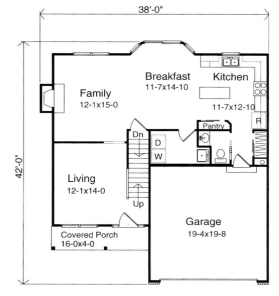

Breakfast
11-7x14-10

Kitchen

Family
12-1x15-0

11-7x12-10

Pantry

R

Dn

D

W

42'-0"

Living
12-1x14-0

Up

Garage
19-4x19-8

Covered Porch
16-0x4-0

First Floor
903 sq. ft.

159

PLAN DETAILS

- 1,640 total square feet of living area
- An open great room and dining area is topped by a stepped ceiling treatment that reaches a 9' height
- The functional kitchen enjoys a walk-in pantry, angles and a delightful snack bar
- Warmth radiates through the combined living areas from the corner fireplace; while a covered porch offers outdoor enjoyment
- 3 bedrooms, 2 baths, 2-car garage
- Basement foundation

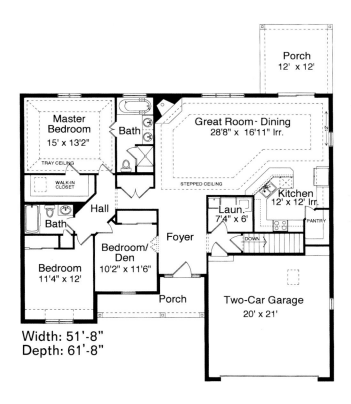

Porch
12' x 12'

Master
Bedroom
15' x 13'2"

TRAY CEILING

Bath

Great Room - Dining
28'8" x 16'11" Irr.

STEPPED CEILING

WALK-IN
CLOSET

Kitchen
12' x 12' Irr.

PANTRY

Bath

Hall

Laun.
7'4" x 6'

DOWN

Foyer

Bedroom/
Den
10'2" x 11'6"

Bedroom
11'4" x 12'

Porch

Two-Car Garage
20' x 21'

Width: 51'-8"
Depth: 61'-8"

PLAN DETAILS

- 1,783 total square feet of living area
- Grand foyer leads to the family room
- Walk-in pantry in the kitchen
- Master bath has a step-down doorless shower, huge vanity and a large walk-in closet
- 3 bedrooms, 2 baths, 2-car garage
- Slab foundation

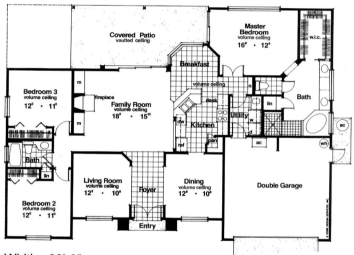

Covered Patio
vaulted ceiling

Master
Bedroom
volume ceiling
16⁸ · 12⁴

w.i.c.

Breakfast
volume ceiling

Bedroom 3
volume ceiling
12⁰ · 11⁰

fireplace

Family Room
volume ceiling
18⁸ · 15⁰

desk

Bath

Utility

Kitchen

dw

Bath

lin

Living Room
volume ceiling
12⁸ · 10⁸

Foyer

Dining
volume ceiling
12⁸ · 10⁸

Double Garage

Bedroom 2
volume ceiling
12⁰ · 11⁰

Entry

Width: 60'-0"
Depth: 45'-0"

PLAN DETAILS

- 2,636 total square feet of living area
- Stunning exterior creates value
- The great room, breakfast room/balcony and kitchen all enjoy views through the two-story window wall of the atrium bay
- The dining room features a handsome tray ceiling and three patio doors to the front porch designed to be fixed or operable
- The master bedroom enjoys a double-door entry, a bay window overlooking the sundeck, a huge walk-in closet and a lavish bath
- 4 bedrooms, 3 1/2 baths, 3-car side entry garage
- Walk-out basement foundation

Rear View

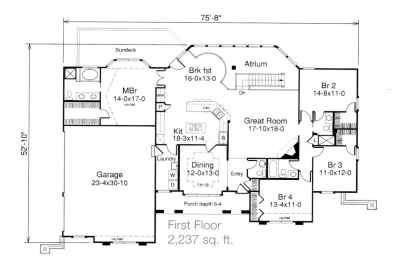

75'-8"

52'-10"

Sundeck

Brk fst
16-0x13-0

Atrium

MBr
14-0x17-0
vaulted

desk

Dn

Br 2
14-8x11-0

Kit
18-3x11-4

P

DW

Great Room
17-10x18-0

R

L

Br 3
11-0x12-0

Laundry

Dining
12-0x13-0
tray clg

Entry

W
D

Garage
23-4x30-10

Br 4
13-4x11-0

Porch depth 6-4

vaulted

First Floor
2,237 sq. ft.

vaulted

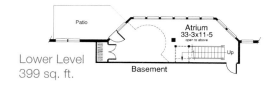

Patio

Atrium
33-3x11-5
open to above

Up

Lower Level
399 sq. ft.

Basement

PLAN DETAILS

- 2,241 total square feet of living area
- Columns define the formal dining room and add to the elegant ambiance
- The inviting living room is warmed by a striking fireplace
- The efficiently designed kitchen features a snack bar that opens to the breakfast area creating a great gathering space
- 4 bedrooms, 2 1/2 baths, 2-car side entry garage
- Slab foundation

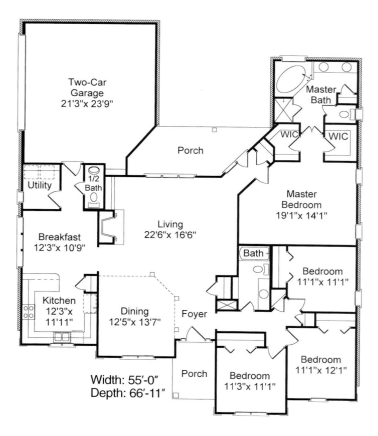

Two-Car Garage
21'3"x 23'9"

Master Bath

WIC   WIC

Porch

Master Bedroom
19'1"x 14'1"

Utility

1/2 Bath

Breakfast
12'3"x 10'9"

Living
22'6"x 16'6"

Bath

Bedroom
11'1"x 11'1"

Kitchen
12'3"x 11'11"

Dining
12'5"x 13'7"

Foyer

Bedroom
11'1"x 12'1"

Width: 55'-0"
Depth: 66'-11"

Porch

Bedroom
11'3"x 11'1"

PLAN DETAILS

- 1,676 total square feet of living area
- The living area skylights and large breakfast room with bay window provide plenty of sunlight
- The master bedroom has a walk-in closet and both the secondary bedrooms have large closets
- Vaulted ceilings, plant shelving and a fireplace provide quality living
- 3 bedrooms, 2 baths, 2-car garage
- Basement foundation, drawings also include crawl space and slab foundations

Rear View

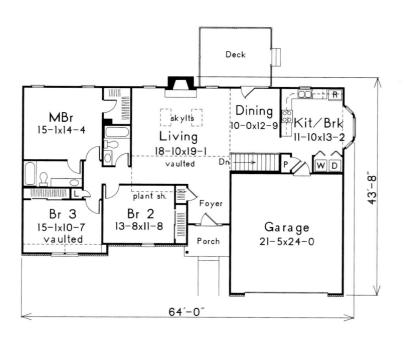

Deck

MBr
15-1x14-4

skylts

Living
18-10x19-1
vaulted

Dining
10-0x12-9

Kit/Brk
11-10x13-2

Dn

R

P

W D

plant sh.

Foyer

Br 3
15-1x10-7
vaulted

Br 2
13-8x11-8

Porch

Garage
21-5x24-0

L

43'-8"

64'-0"

PLAN DETAILS

- 1,084 total square feet of living area
- Delightful country porch for quiet evenings
- The living room offers a front feature window which invites the sun and includes a fireplace and dining area with private patio
- The U-shaped kitchen features lots of cabinets and a bayed breakfast room with built-in pantry
- Both bedrooms have walk-in closets and access to their own bath
- 2 bedrooms, 2 baths
- Basement foundation

Rear View

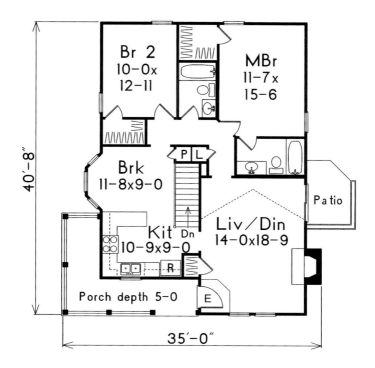

Br 2
10-0x
12-11

MBr
11-7x
15-6

Brk
11-8x9-0

P L

Dn

Kit
10-9x9-0

Liv/Din
14-0x18-9

Patio

R

E

Porch depth 5-0

40'-8"

35'-0"

PLAN DETAILS

- 1,670 total square feet of living area
- Lots of closet space throughout
- Family room is flooded with sunlight from many windows
- Open living areas make this home appear larger
- 4 bedrooms, 2 1/2 baths, 2-car garage
- Basement foundation

Second Floor
692 sq. ft.

Bedroom 2
9^4 • 12^{10}

Bedroom 3
10^0 • 10^0

w.i.c.

lin

Bath

Bath

down

Master Bedroom
16^0 • 10^6

w.i.c.

First Floor
978 sq. ft.

Dining
9^0 • 12^0

Kitchen

dw

Breakfast

fireplace

Family Room
12^8 • 16^8

ref   desk

Pdr.

dn   dn

Living Room
16^0 • 18^4

up

Double Garage

Entry

up

Width: 40'-0"
Depth: 39'-8"

PLAN DETAILS

- 1,525 total square feet of living area
- The kitchen is enhanced with an open bar that connects the great room
- A corner gas fireplace warms the entire living area
- The master suite features a whirlpool tub flanked by walk-in closets
- 3 bedrooms, 2 baths, 2-car garage
- Slab, crawl space, basement or walk-out basement foundation, please specify when ordering

51'-6"

49'-10"

WHP TUB

M. BATH
15'-8" X 10'-8"

LIN

MASTER SUITE
15'-8" X 12'-0"
9' BOXED CEILING

COVERED PORCH
24'-10" X 9'-8"

ATRIUM DOOR

GAS FIREPLACE

OPEN BAR

GREAT ROOM
13'-6" X 19'-8"
9' BOXED CEILING

DINING ROOM
11'-0" X 9'-6"

KITCHEN
15'-2" X 10'-8"

DW

REF

RG

GRILLING PATIO
10'-4" X 9'-8"

BRKFAST ROOM
10'-0" X 8'-0"

COMPUTER DESK

BATH

LAU.
6'-4" X 5'-6"

WH

D

W

FOYER
6'-6" X 7'-0"

OPT DOOR

BEDROOM 3 / STUDY
10'-0" X 10'-8"

LIN

BEDROOM 2
10'-2" X 10'-8"

GARAGE
20'-10" X 20'-0"

COVERED PORCH
16'-5" X 5'-0"

© 1998 NELSON DESIGN GROUP, LLC.

175

PLAN NUMBER: 586-048D-0008

PRICE CODE: C

PLAN DETAILS

- 2,089 total square feet of living area
- Family room features a fireplace, built-in bookshelves and triple sliders opening to the covered patio
- Kitchen overlooks the family room and features a pantry and desk
- Separated from the three secondary bedrooms, the master bedroom becomes a quiet retreat with patio access
- Master bedroom features an oversized bath with walk-in closet and corner tub
- 4 bedrooms, 3 baths, 2-car garage
- Slab foundation

Rear View

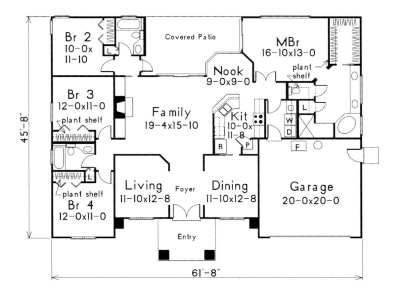

Br 2
10-0x
11-10

Covered Patio

MBr
16-10x13-0

plant
shelf

Nook
9-0x9-0

Br 3
12-0x11-0

Family
19-4x15-10

Kit
10-0x
11-8

plant shelf

R

P

F

W

D

L

plant shelf

Br 4
12-0x11-0

Living
11-10x12-8

Foyer

Dining
11-10x12-8

Garage
20-0x20-0

Entry

45'-8"

61'-8"

PLAN DETAILS

- 1,587 total square feet of living area
- The spacious family room features a vaulted ceiling, fireplace and convenient coat closet
- The kitchen/breakfast area is brightened by a large window and includes a convenient pantry
- Secondary bedrooms are generously sized and share a full bath
- 3 bedrooms, 2 baths, 2-car garage
- Basement foundation

Rear View

49'-0"

45'-4"

Kit/Brk
10x18-5

R

P

Family
18x18-6
Vaulted Clg.

MBr
11x15
Vaulted Clg.

L

S W D

Laundry

Br 3
10x11-5

Br 2
11x10

L

Garage
20x19

16x7 Gar. Door

179

PLAN DETAILS

- 1,832 total square feet of living area
- Two-story foyer is a welcoming entry
- All bedrooms are located on the second floor for privacy
- Formal dining room has direct access into the kitchen
- 3 bedrooms, 2 1/2 baths, 2-car garage
- Walk-out basement foundation

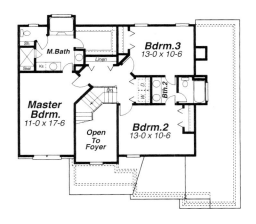

M.Bath

Sh.

Seat   Ks.

Master Bdrm.
11-0 x 17-6

Bdrm.3
13-0 x 10-6

Linen

Dn.

Open To Foyer

W. D.

Bth.2

Bdrm.2
13-0 x 10-6

Second Floor
963 sq. ft.

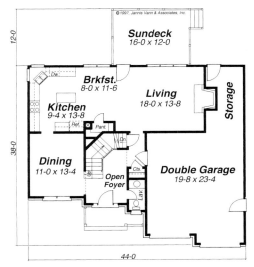

© 1997, Jannis Vann & Associates, Inc.

12-0

Sundeck
16-0 x 12-0

Dw.

Brkfst.
8-0 x 11-6

Living
18-0 x 13-8

Storage

Kitchen
9-4 x 13-8

Ref.   Pant.

38-0

Dn.

Dining
11-0 x 13-4

Open Foyer

Cts.

Lav.

Double Garage
19-8 x 23-4

44-0

First Floor
869 sq. ft.

PLAN DETAILS

- 1,680 total square feet of living area
- Enormous and luxurious master suite
- Kitchen and dining room have vaulted ceilings creating an open feeling
- Double sinks grace secondary bath
- 3 bedrooms, 2 baths, 2-car garage
- Walk-out basement, basement, crawl space or slab foundation, please specify when ordering

51' 6"

COVERED
GRILLING
PORCH
17'-4" X 9'-4"

MASTER
SUITE
20'-10" X 13'-0"
9' PAN CEILING

BEDROOM 2
12'-4" X 10'-0"

GLASS
SHWR

LIN

GREAT ROOM
17'-0" X 20'-0"
9' PAN CEILING

LAU.
5'-8" X 6'-2"

WHP
TUB

GLASS
BLOCKS

BATH

LIN

D

W

DN

OPTIONAL BASEMENT PLAN

52' 4"

GARAGE
20'-10" X 20'-0"

REF PAN

RG

KITCHEN
12'-0" X 12'-0"

FOYER

BEDROOM 3
12'-4" X 11'-8"

DW

PRCH

© 2000 NELSON DESIGN GROUP, LLC

DINING
12'-0" X 10'-0"

VAULTED
CEILING

PLAN DETAILS

- 2,391 total square feet of living area
- Stucco, brick and quoins combine to create a beautiful facade
- The spacious foyer and formal dining room are topped with 12' ceilings
- The grand fireplace flanked by built-in shelves warms the living room, adjoining breakfast area and kitchen
- 4 bedrooms, 3 baths, 2-car side entry garage
- Slab foundation

WIC

WIC

Master
Bath

Porch
26'4"x 9'

Bedroom
11'5"x 11'3"

Master
Bedroom
15'6"x 16'

Living
15'6"x 19'6"

Breakfast
12'x 11'

Bath

Bath

Kitchen
12'x 15'4"

Bedroom
8'x 11'3"

Hall

Foyer
7'x 12'

Dining
12'x 14'

Utility

WIC

Bedroom
11'6"x 14'6"

Two Car
Garage
21'8"x 23'10"

Width: 61'-10"
Depth: 59'-11"

185

PLAN DETAILS

- 1,217 total square feet of living area
- Step up into the main level to see an elegant family room with vaulted ceiling and grand fireplace flanked by windows
- The kitchen/breakfast area enjoys a bright bay window with access to the outdoors
- The master bedroom enjoys a walk-in closet, whirlpool tub and a double vanity
- 3 bedrooms, 2 baths, 2-car garage
- Basement foundation

First Floor
1,217 sq. ft.

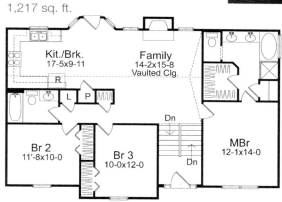

Kit./Brk.
17-5x9-11

Family
14-2x15-8
Vaulted Clg.

R

L P

Dn

Br 2
11'-8x10-0

Br 3
10-0x12-0

Dn

MBr
12-1x14-0

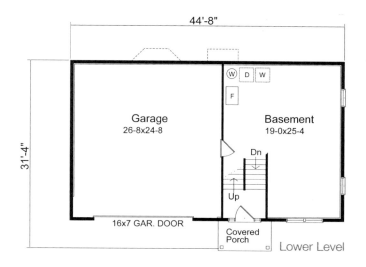

44'-8"

31'-4"

W D W

F

Garage
26-8x24-8

Basement
19-0x25-4

Dn

Up

16x7 GAR. DOOR

Covered
Porch

Lower Level

PLAN DETAILS

- 1,727 total square feet of living area
- The breakfast bay and entry to the covered porch create a bright and cheery place to start the day
- A furniture alcove adds space to the formal dining room
- A rear entry hall offers storage closets and a large laundry room
- All bedrooms are located on the second floor for extra privacy
- 3 bedrooms, 2 1/2 baths, 2-car garage
- Basement foundation

Second Floor
786 sq. ft.

Bedroom
11'3" x 11'6"

Bath

Great Room
Below

TRAY CEILING

Master
Bedroom
12'2" x 16'

DOWN

Hall

Foyer
Below

Bath

PLANT SHELF

Bedroom
11'6" x 9'7"

WALK-IN
CLOSET

SLOPE   SLOPE

ATTIC
STORAGE

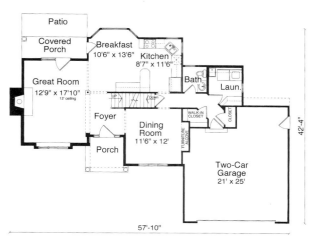

Patio

Covered
Porch

Breakfast
10'6" x 13'6"

Kitchen
8'7" x 11'6"

Bath

Laun.

Great Room
12'9" x 17'10"
12' ceiling

WALK-IN
CLOSET

CLOSET

Foyer

Dining
Room
11'6" x 12'

UP

FURNITURE
ALCOVE

Porch

Two-Car
Garage
21' x 25'

42'-4"

57'-10"

First Floor
941 sq. ft.

PLAN DETAILS

- 988 total square feet of living area
- Pleasant covered porch entry
- The kitchen, living and dining areas are combined to maximize space
- The entry has a convenient coat closet
- Laundry closet is located adjacent to the bedrooms
- 3 bedrooms, 1 bath, 1-car garage
- Basement foundation, drawings also include crawl space foundation

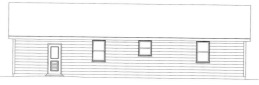

Rear View

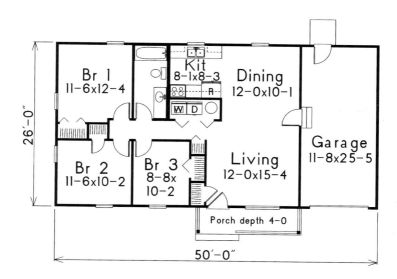

Br 1
11-6x12-4

Kit
8-1x8-3

Dining
12-0x10-1

Garage
11-8x25-5

Br 2
11-6x10-2

Br 3
8-8x
10-2

Living
12-0x15-4

26'-0"

Porch depth 4-0

50'-0"

PLAN DETAILS

- 1,161 total square feet of living area
- Brickwork and feature window add elegance to this home for a narrow lot
- Living room enjoys a vaulted ceiling, fireplace and opens to kitchen
- U-shaped kitchen offers a breakfast area with bay window, snack bar and built-in pantry
- 3 bedrooms, 2 baths
- Basement foundation

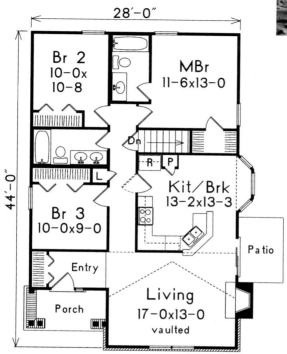

28'-0"

44'-0"

Br 2
10-0x
10-8

MBr
11-6x13-0

B

Dn

R P

Kit/Brk
13-2x13-3

L

Br 3
10-0x9-0

Patio

Entry

Living
17-0x13-0
vaulted

Porch

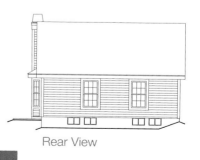

Rear View

PLAN DETAILS

- 1,902 total square feet of living area
- Wrap-around kitchen counter plus an island provides plenty of counterspace
- The foyer opens into the expansive vaulted great room providing an impressive entrance
- The laundry area conveniently includes a half bath and walk-in closet
- 3 bedrooms, 2 1/2 baths, 3-car garage
- Basement foundation

71'-0"

44'-4"

MBr
15-4x15-4

Great Rm.
20-0x20-11

Kit./Brkf.
20-7x13-4
Vaulted Clg.

Desk

L

Dn

Laundry

Foyer

Garage
20-4x33-0

Br 3
12-11x12-1

Br 2
12-8x12-1

Porch

PLAN NUMBER: 586-055D-0209

PRICE CODE: D

PLAN DETAILS

- 2,029 total square feet of living area
- The bedrooms are located away from main living areas for privacy
- The kitchen easily serves the formal dining room, breakfast room and grilling porch
- Fireplaces in the great room and hearth room warm the entire home
- Optional second floor has an additional 754 square feet of living area
- 3 bedrooms, 2 baths, 2-car side entry garage
- Slab, crawl space, basement or walk-out basement foundation, please specify when ordering

Optional
Second Floor
754 sq. ft.

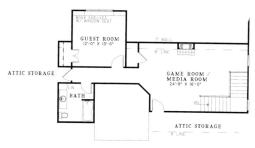

BOOK SHELVES
W/ WINDOW SEAT

GUEST ROOM
12'-0" X 13'-0"

7' WALL

8' LINE

ATTIC STORAGE

GAME ROOM /
MEDIA ROOM
24'-8" X 16'-0"

BATH

LIN

DN

ATTIC STORAGE
8' LINE

66'-4"

58'-7"

WHP
TUB

M.
BATH
15'-4" X 12'-8"

LIN

SHWR

BATH

MASTER
SUITE
13'-6" X 16'-4"
10' BOXED CEILING

GREAT ROOM
13'-10" X 19'-2"

8' ROUND COLUMNS

GRILLING
PORCH
BEADED CEILING
26'-10" X 8'-0"

BREAKFAST
ROOM
12'-10" X 12'-3"

HEARTH
ROOM
11'-10" X 16'-5"

TO BONUS
AREA ABOVE

KITCHEN
11'-8" X 12'-9"

REF
DW

PANTRY

LAU.
8'-6" X 5'-10"

W

BEDROOM 3
10'-8" X 11'-0"

BEDROOM 2 /
STUDY
11'-2" X 11'-2"

LIN

FOYER

8' ROUND COLUMNS

DINING ROOM
12'-4" X 13'-4"
10' CEILING

UP
DN

ATTIC
ACCESS

COVERED
PORCH
21'-6" X 12'-6"
10' BEADED CEILING

GARAGE
22'-0" X 23'-6"

10" ROUND COLUMNS

First Floor
2,029 sq. ft.

PLAN DETAILS

- 1,519 total square feet of living area
- The large living room boasts a vaulted ceiling with plant shelf, fireplace, and opens to the bayed dining area
- The kitchen has an adjoining laundry/mud room and features a vaulted ceiling, snack counter and a built-in pantry
- Two walk-in closets, a stylish bath and small sitting area accompany the master bedroom
- 4 bedrooms, 2 baths, 2-car garage
- Crawl space foundation, drawings also include slab and basement foundations

Rear View

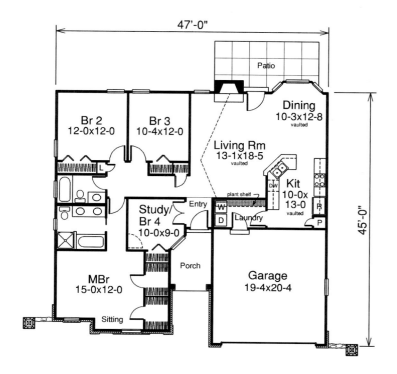

47'-0"

Patio

Br 2
12-0x12-0

Br 3
10-4x12-0

Dining
10-3x12-8
vaulted

Living Rm
13-1x18-5
vaulted

plant shelf

Kit
10-0x
13-0
vaulted

DW

W

D

Entry

Study/
Br 4
10-0x9-0

Laundry

R

P

MBr
15-0x12-0

Porch

Garage
19-4x20-4

Sitting

45'-0"

PLAN DETAILS

- 1,798 total square feet of living area
- The expansive great room enjoys a fireplace and has access onto the rear patio
- The centrally located kitchen is easily accessible to the dining room and breakfast area
- The master bedroom boasts a sloped ceiling and deluxe bath with a corner whirlpool tub and large walk-in closet
- A screened porch offers relaxing outdoor living
- 3 bedrooms, 2 baths, 2-car garage
- Basement foundation

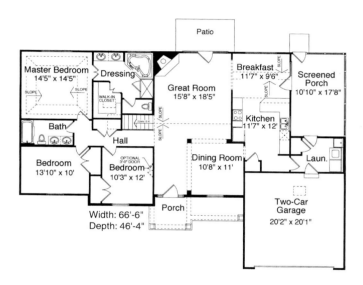

Patio

Master Bedroom
14'5" x 14'5"

SLOPE SLOPE

Dressing

WALK-IN CLOSET

Bath

Hall

Bedroom
13'10" x 10'

OPTIONAL
3'-0" DOOR
Bedroom
10'3" x 12'

Great Room
15'8" x 18'5"

SLOPE SLOPE

Breakfast
11'7" x 9'6"

SLOPE

Screened
Porch
10'10" x 17'8"

SLOPE

Kitchen
11'7" x 12'

Dining Room
10'8" x 11'

Laun.

Porch

Two-Car
Garage
20'2" x 20'1"

Width: 66'-6"
Depth: 46'-4"

PLAN NUMBER: 586-058D-0038
PRICE CODE: B

PLAN DETAILS

- 1,680 total square feet of living area
- Compact and efficient layout in an affordable package
- Second floor has three bedrooms all with oversized closets
- All bedrooms are on the second floor for privacy
- 3 bedrooms, 2 1/2 baths, 2-car garage
- Basement foundation

202

Second Floor
784 sq. ft.

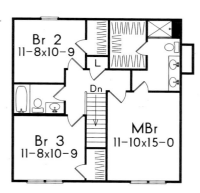

Br 2
11-8x10-9

L

Dn

MBr
11-10x15-0

Br 3
11-8x10-9

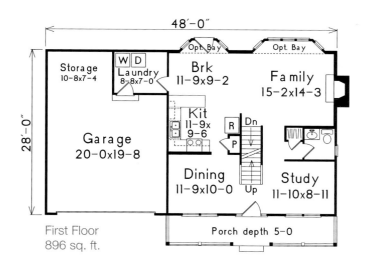

48'-0"

Opt. Bay   Opt. Bay

Storage
10-8x7-4

W D
Laundry
8-8x7-0

Brk
11-9x9-2

Family
15-2x14-3

28'-0"

Kit
11-9x
9-6

Garage
20-0x19-8

R Dn

P

Dining
11-9x10-0   Up

Study
11-10x8-11

First Floor
896 sq. ft.

Porch depth 5-0

203

PLAN DETAILS

- 2,420 total square feet of living area
- The huge great room has a fireplace with flanking shelves, a wide bay window and dining area surrounded with windows
- Kitchen has a corner window sink, island snack bar, walk-in pantry and breakfast area with adjoining covered patio
- 1,014 square feet of optional living area on the lower level includes a large family room with fireplace and home theater room with walk-in bar and half bath
- 4 bedrooms, 3 1/2 baths, 2-car side entry garage
- Basement foundation

First Floor
2,420 sq. ft.

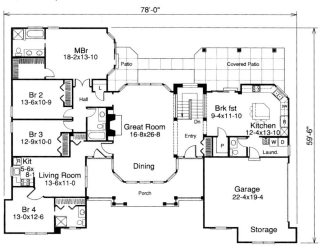

78'-0"

59'-6"

MBr
18-2x13-10

Patio

Covered Patio

Br 2
13-6x10-9

Hall

Great Room
16-8x26-8

Entry

Dn

Brk fst
9-4x11-10

Kitchen
12-4x13-10

DW

Br 3
12-9x10-0

Kit
5-6x
8-1

Living Room
13-6x11-0

Dining

Porch

P

S W D

Laund.

Br 4
13-0x12-6

Garage
22-4x19-4

Storage

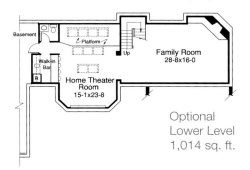

Basement

Platform

Up

Family Room
28-8x16-0

Walk-in
Bar

Home Theater
Room
15-1x23-8

Optional
Lower Level
1,014 sq. ft.

PLAN DETAILS

- 1,927 total square feet of living area
- Bedrooms are secluded on one side of the home
- The kitchen includes a wrap-around counter with seating and opens to the dining room and breakfast room
- Optional second floor has an additional 909 square feet of living space
- 3 bedrooms, 2 baths, 2-car rear entry garage
- Slab, crawl space, basement or walk-out basement foundation, please specify when ordering

39'-0"

82'-4"

GARAGE
20'-0" X 20'-0"

© 1998 NELSON DESIGN GROUP, LLC

MASTER
SUITE
12'-4" X 19'-0"
11" BOXED CEILING

STORAGE
BINS

16" WIDE BENCH
W/ STORAGE

KID'S NOOK   LAU.
7'-8" X 8'-0"

STRG.

W.

MEDIA
CENTER

LIN

GAS
FIREPLACE

ATRIUM
DOORS

M.BATH
12'-4" X 15'-0"

GREAT RM.
17'-8" X 18'-0"

GRILLING
PORCH
8'-0" X 16'-0"

WHP
TUB

GLASS
SHWR

TO ATTIC
STORAGE OR
BONUS ROOM
UP

BEDROOM 2
12'-4" X 12'-0"

DW

BREAKFAST
ROOM
7'-8" X 15'-0"

KITCHEN
10'-0" X 12'-0"

COMPUTER
CENTER

REF   PANTRY

LIN

BATH

8" RND.
COLUMNS

FOYER
6'-0" X 12'-0"

DINING
ROOM
11'-0" X 12'-0"

BEDROOM 3
12'-4" X 14'-4"

8' COVERED
PORCH

12" COLUMNS

First Floor
1,927 sq. ft.

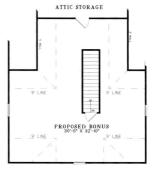

ATTIC STORAGE

9' LINE

9' LINE

PROPOSED BONUS
30'-0" X 32'-10"

9' LINE

9' LINE

Optional
Second Floor
909 sq. ft.

207

PLAN DETAILS

- 1,970 total square feet of living area
- A covered porch and dormers accentuate the facade of this duplex making it appear as a single-family home
- The U-shaped kitchen offers plenty of room for dining with a snack bar and adjoining breakfast room which opens to the patio
- A large laundry room adds convenience to this charming duplex home
- Each unit has 2 bedrooms, 1 bath, optional 2-car garage
- Slab or crawl space foundation, please specify when ordering
- Duplex has 985 square feet of living area per unit

208

54'-0"

65'-2"

OPTIONAL GARAGE
18'-4" X 20'-0"

OPTIONAL GARAGE
18'-4" X 20'-0"

PATIO

PATIO

STRG

BRKFST RM.
14'-8" X 15'-0"
42' HIGH BAR

BRKFST RM.
14'-8" X 15'-0"
42' HIGH BAR

STRG

LAU.
6'-4" X 7'-10"

LAU.
6'-4" X 7'-10"

KIT.

KIT.

BEDROOM 2
11'-4" X 11'-0"

BEDROOM 2
11'-4" X 11'-0"

BATH

GREAT RM.
14'-8" X 16'-6"

GREAT RM.
14'-8" X 16'-6"

BATH

OPT GAS FIREPLACE

OPT GAS FIREPLACE

COVERED PORCH
30'-0" X 8'-0"

10" RND COL

BEDROOM 1
11'-4" X 11'-0"

BEDROOM 1
11'-4" X 11'-0"

209

PLAN DETAILS

- 1,668 total square feet of living area
- Easy access from garage into home
- Bath includes a tub as well as a separate shower
- Large living area combines with dining room making a nice area for entertaining
- Each unit has 2 bedrooms, 1 bath, 1-car garage
- Basement foundation
- Duplex has 834 square feet of living space per unit

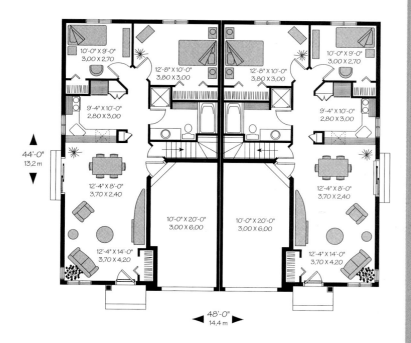

10'-0" X 9'-0"
3,00 X 2,70

12'-8" X 10'-0"
3,80 X 3,00

12'-8" X 10'-0"
3,80 X 3,00

10'-0" X 9'-0"
3,00 X 2,70

9'-4" X 10'-0"
2,80 X 3,00

9'-4" X 10'-0"
2,80 X 3,00

44'-0"
13,2 m

12'-4" X 8'-0"
3,70 X 2,40

12'-4" X 8'-0"
3,70 X 2,40

10'-0" X 20'-0"
3,00 X 6,00

10'-0" X 20'-0"
3,00 X 6,00

12'-4" X 14'-0"
3,70 X 4,20

12'-4" X 14'-0"
3,70 X 4,20

48'-0"
14,4 m

PLAN DETAILS

- 2,885 total square feet of living area
- Cozy study adjoins the master bedroom
- Several windows brighten the main living area
- Counterspace in the kitchen overlooks the dining and living areas
- Convenient laundry closet is on the second floor
- Each unit has 3 bedrooms, 3 baths
- Slab foundation
- Unit A has 1,437 square feet of living space and Unit B has 1,448 square feet of living space

Unit B
Second Floor
645 sq. ft.

Unit A
Second
Floor
634 sq. ft.

Unit A
First Floor
803 sq. ft.

Unit B
First Floor
803 sq. ft.

Rear View

PLAN DETAILS

- 1,700 total square feet of living area
- Front facade fits splendidly with residential surroundings
- Well-planned kitchen includes an abundance of cabinets
- Spacious bedroom with double closets
- Plant shelf, open stairway and vaulted ceilings highlight living space
- Convenient entrance from garage into main living area
- Each unit has 2 bedrooms, 1 bath, 1-car side entry garage
- Basement foundation
- Duplex has 850 square feet of living space per unit

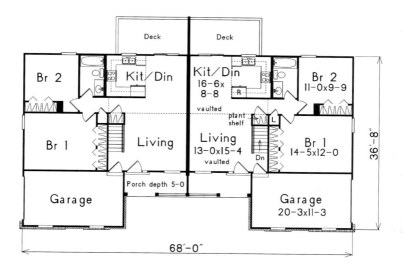

Deck   Deck

Br 2

Kit/Din

Kit/Din
16-6x
8-8

Br 2
11-0x9-9

vaulted

plant
shelf

Br 1

Living

Living
13-0x15-4

Br 1
14-5x12-0

vaulted

Dn

Porch depth 5-0

Garage

Garage
20-3x11-3

36'-8"

68'-0"

Rear View

PLAN DETAILS

- 3,366 total square feet of living area
- 9' ceilings throughout the first floor
- Impressive kitchen with center island/snack bar has lots of counterspace and cabinetry
- Master suite has a private bath and is located on the first floor
- Bonus room has an additional 265 square feet of living area per unit
- Each unit has 3 bedrooms, 2 1/2 baths, 1-car garage
- Crawl space or slab foundation, please specify when ordering
- Duplex has 1,683 square feet of living space per unit

Second Floor
529 sq. ft.
per unit

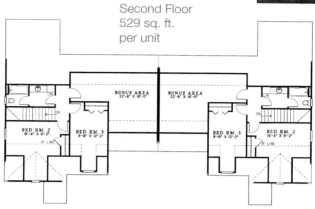

BONUS AREA
22'-6" X 16'-0"

BONUS AREA
22'-6" X 16'-0"

BED RM. 2
16'-4" X 9'-2"

BED RM. 3
9'-8" X 12'-2"

BED RM. 3
9'-8" X 12'-2"

BED RM. 2
16'-4" X 9'-2"

80' 0"

GLASS BLOCKS

MASTER BATH
16'-8" X 9'-0"

GRILLING PORCH
14'-0" X 6'-0"

GRILLING PORCH
14'-0" X 6'-0"

MASTER BATH
16'-8" X 9'-0"

GLASS BLOCKS

LAU. D
9'-6" X 6'-0"

LAU.
9'-6" X 6'-0"

KITCHEN
17'-0" X 10'-0"

NOOK
7'-0" X 9'-0"

NOOK
7'-0" X 9'-0"

KITCHEN
17'-0" X 10'-0"

MASTER SUITE
17'-8" X 14'-0"

ISLAND

ISLAND

MASTER SUITE
17'-8" X 14'-0"

GARAGE
12'-8" X 19'-4"

GARAGE
12'-8" X 19'-4"

50' 0"

GAS FIREPLACE

8" COLUMNS

© 2000 NELSON DESIGN GROUP, LLC

8" COLUMNS

GAS FIREPLACE

GREAT RM.
15'-6" X 16'-0"

DINING
10'-2" X 14'-0"

DINING
10'-2" X 14'-0"

GREAT RM.
15'-6" X 16'-0"

FOYER

FOYER

PRCH

PRCH

26' 0"

First Floor
1,154 sq. ft.
per unit

PLAN DETAILS

- 2,986 total square feet of living area
- First floor units have access to their own sundecks while lower level units each enjoy a private patio
- Each unit features a hookup for a stacked washer and dryer
- Units A and B have 2 bedrooms, 1 bath and Units C and D have 1 bedroom, 1 bath
- Walk-out basement foundation with centrally located storage area
- Fourplex has 1,574 square feet of living area on the first floor and 1,412 square feet of living area on the lower level

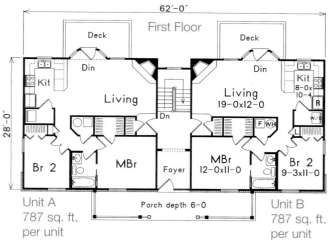

First Floor

62'-0"

Deck

Din

Kit

Living

Dn

MBr

Foyer

Br 2

28'-0"

Deck

Din

Living
19-0x12-0

F WH

MBr
12-0x11-0

Kit
8-0x
10-4

R

W/

L

Br 2
9-3x11-0

Porch depth 6-0

Unit A
787 sq. ft.
per unit

Unit B
787 sq. ft.
per unit

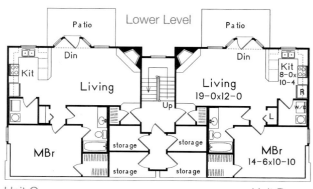

Lower Level

Patio

Din

Kit

Living

Up

MBr

storage

storage

Patio

Din

Living
19-0x12-0

MBr
14-6x10-10

Kit
8-0x
10-4

R

W/

L

storage

storage

Unit C
706 sq. ft.
per unit

Unit D
706 sq. ft.
per unit

PLAN DETAILS

- 4,184 total square feet of living area
- Combined kitchen, living and dining rooms create an open living atmosphere
- Handy laundry room and large linen closet on the second floor
- Master bedroom includes a private bath and balcony
- First floor bedroom is an ideal guest room
- Each unit has 4 bedrooms, 3 baths
- Slab foundation
- Duplex has 2,092 square feet of living space per unit with 1,108 square feet on the first floor and 984 square feet on the second floor

Second Floor
984 sq. ft.
per unit

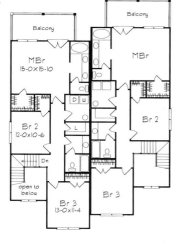

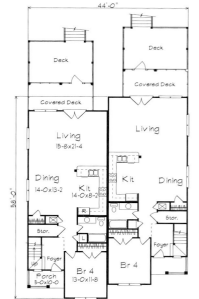

First Floor
1,108 sq. ft. per unit

PLAN DETAILS

- 3,218 total square feet of living area
- Luxurious master bath contains an oversized whirlpool tub with glass block wall
- Unique golf cart storage is an added bonus in the garage
- Two second floor bedrooms share a bath
- Each unit has 3 bedrooms, 2 1/2 baths, 2-car garage
- Crawl space or slab foundation, please specify when ordering
- Duplex has 1,609 square feet of living space per unit

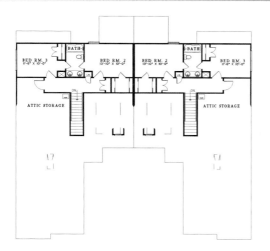

Second Floor
478 sq. ft.
per unit

First Floor
1,131 sq. ft.
per unit

223

PLAN DETAILS

- 2,318 total square feet of living area
- Great room and dining area are complemented with a fireplace and patio access
- Breakfast bar has corner sink which overlooks great room
- Plant shelf graces vaulted entry
- Master bedroom provides walk-in closet and private bath
- Each unit has 3 bedrooms, 2 baths, 1-car garage
- Basement foundation
- Duplex has 1,159 square feet of living space per unit

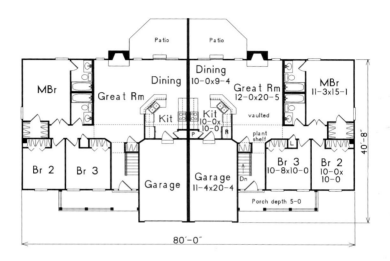

Patio   Patio

MBr

Great Rm

Dining

Dining
10-0x9-4

Great Rm
12-0x20-5

MBr
11-3x15-1

vaulted

Kit
10-0x
10-0

Kit
10-0x
10-0

plant shelf

Br 2   Br 3

Garage

Garage
11-4x20-4

Dn

Br 3
10-8x10-0

Br 2
10-0x
10-0

Porch depth 5-0

40'-8"

80'-0"

Rear View

PLAN DETAILS

- 2,558 total square feet of living area
- A 10' boxed ceiling, gas fireplace and decorative columns in the combined great room and dining room are elegant touches to this compact duplex
- The cozy nook is a great place to start the day with a bright, cheerful window letting in the sunlight
- Each unit has 3 bedrooms, 2 baths, 2-car garage
- Slab or crawl space foundation, please specify when ordering
- Duplex has 1,279 square feet of living area per unit

88'-0"

54'-8"

BEDROOM 2
10'-6" X 11'-3"

MASTER
SUITE
11'-0" X 14'-8"
10' BOXED
CEILING

BEDROOM 3 /
OFFICE
10'-6" X 9'-3"

GARAGE
17'-8" X 20'-0"

© 2000 NELSON DESIGN GROUP, LLC.

GARAGE
17'-8" X 20'-0"

MASTER
SUITE
11'-0" X 14'-8"
10' BOXED
CEILING

BEDROOM 2
10'-6" X 11'-3"

BEDROOM 3 /
OFFICE
10'-6" X 9'-3"

8' BOXED
COLUMNS

DINING RM.
10'-2" X 11'-10"

GREAT RM.
14'-6" X 17'-0"
GAS
FIREPLACE

10' BOXED CEILING

FOYER

KIT.
10'-6" X 16'-10"

COVERED PORCH
16'-0" X 8'-0"

NOOK

8' BOXED
COLUMNS

DINING RM.
10'-2" X 11'-10"

GREAT RM.
14'-6" X 17'-0"
GAS
FIREPLACE

10' BOXED CEILING

FOYER

KIT.
10'-6" X 16'-10"

COVERED PORCH
16'-0" X 8'-0"

NOOK

PLAN DETAILS

- 3,648 total square feet of living area
- Kitchen is open to the breakfast area
- Spacious bath includes a laundry closet
- Sitting area is cozy and separate from other areas
- Each unit has 2 bedrooms, 1 bath
- Slab foundation
- Duplex has 912 square feet of living space per unit

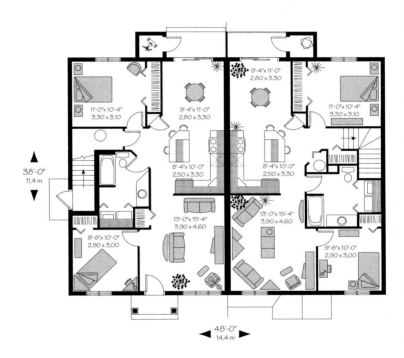

11'-0"x 10'-4"
3,30 x 3,10

9'-4"x 11'-0"
2,80 x 3,30

9'-4"x 11'-0"
2,80 x 3,30

9'-4"x 11'-0"
2,80 x 3,30

11'-0"x 10'-4"
3,30 x 3,10

8'-4"x 10'-0"
2,50 x 3,30

8'-4"x 10'-0"
2,50 x 3,30

13'-0"x 15'-4"
3,90 x 4,60

13'-0"x 15'-4"
3,90 x 4,60

9'-8"x 10'-0"
2,90 x 3,00

9'-8"x 10'-0"
2,90 x 3,00

38'-0"
11,4 m

48'-0"
14,4 m

PLAN DETAILS

- 1,656 total square feet of living area
- The front porch opens to the grand living room which features access to the rear patio
- The efficiently designed kitchen spills into the dining room
- Spacious bedrooms remain private from the living areas
- Each unit has 2 bedrooms, 1 bath
- Crawl space foundation, drawings also include slab foundation
- Duplex has 828 square feet of living area per unit

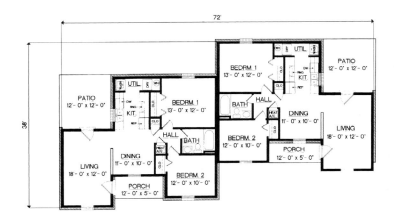

72'

38'

PATIO
12'- 0" x 12'- 0"

UTIL.

BEDRM. 1
13'- 0" x 12'- 0"

KIT.

CLO

HALL

BATH

DINING
11'- 0" x 10'- 0"

LIVING
18'- 0" x 12'- 0"

HEAT
A/C

BEDRM. 2
12'- 0" x 10'- 0"

PORCH
12'- 0" x 5'- 0"

BEDRM. 1
13'- 0" x 12'- 0"

UTIL.

KIT.

CLO

BATH

HALL

HEAT
A/C

DINING
11'- 0" x 10'- 0"

BEDRM. 2
12'- 0" x 10'- 0"

PORCH
12'- 0" x 5'- 0"

PATIO
12'- 0" x 12'- 0"

LIVING
18'- 0" x 12'- 0"

PLAN DETAILS

- 3,258 total square feet of living area
- Multi-gables, brickwork, windows with shutters and planter boxes create great curb appeal
- Well-equipped kitchen includes an island snack bar, bayed breakfast room, built-in pantry, corner windows above sink and laundry room
- Second floor has large bedrooms including a vaulted master bedroom with luxury bath
- Each unit has 3 bedrooms, 2 1/2 baths, 2-car garage
- Basement foundation
- Duplex has 1,629 square feet of living space per unit

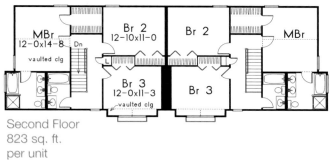

Second Floor
823 sq. ft.
per unit

MBr
12-0x14-8

Br 2
12-10x11-0

Br 2

MBr

vaulted clg

Dn

L

Br 3
12-0x11-3

Br 3

vaulted clg

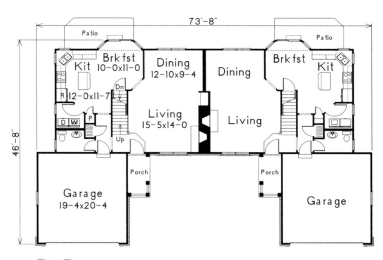

73'-8"

46'-8"

Patio

Patio

Kit

Brkfst
10-0x11-0

Dining
12-10x9-4

Dining

Brkfst

Kit

R 12-0x11-7

Dn

Living
15-5x14-0

Living

D W

P

Up

Porch

Porch

Garage
19-4x20-4

Garage

First Floor
806 sq. ft.
per unit

PLAN NUMBER: 586-025D-0061

PRICE CODE: H

PLAN DETAILS

- 5,516 total square feet of living area
- All master bedrooms have a private bath and walk-in closet
- Unit A has 1,341 square feet of living space with 2 bedrooms, 2 1/2 baths, 1-car garage
- Unit B has 1,120 square feet of living space with 2 bedrooms, 2 baths, 1-car garage
- Unit C has 1,511 square feet of living space with 2 bedrooms, 2 1/2 baths, 1-car garage
- Unit D has 1,544 square feet of living space with 3 bedrooms, 2 1/2 baths, 1-car garage
- Slab foundation

Unit A First Floor 764 sq. ft.

Unit A Second Floor 577 sq. ft.

Unit B 1,120 sq. ft.

Unit C First Floor 983 sq. ft.

Unit C Second Floor 528 sq. ft.

Unit D First Floor 788 sq. ft.

Unit D Second Floor 756 sq. ft.

PLAN DETAILS

- 2,426 total square feet of living area
- Angled entry leads into the combined dining and living rooms
- Master bedroom enjoys a vaulted ceiling, private bath and walk-in closet
- Efficiently designed kitchen includes space for a washer and dryer
- Each unit has 2 bedrooms, 2 baths, 2-car garage
- Basement foundation
- Duplex has 1,213 square feet of living area per unit

64'-2"

70'-7"

M. BR.
13/1X15/10
VLTD' CLG.

LIVING
14/9X16/0

DINING
12/6X10/0

ENTRY

BR. #2
10/0X11/11

KIT
13/8X10/6

GARAGE
19/5X19/5

237

PLAN DETAILS

- 2,910 total square feet of living area
- Sunny breakfast room is adjacent to kitchen and has access to an outdoor covered grilling porch
- Master suite has an intricate ceiling and a private luxurious bath with double closets
- Each unit has 3 bedrooms, 2 baths, 1-car garage
- Crawl space or slab foundation, please specify when ordering
- Duplex has 1,455 square feet of living space per unit

80' 8"

63' 4"

MASTER
BATH
15'-8" X 11'-4"

WHP
TUB

GRILLING
PORCH
12'-0" X 6'-0"

MASTER
SUITE
10' BOXED CEILING
15'-8" X 13'-8"

BRKFAST
RM.
11'-4" X 12'-0"

STORAGE
7'-2" X 3'-0"

STORAGE
7'-2" X 3'-0"

GRILLING
PORCH
12'-0" X 6'-0"

WHP
TUB

MASTER
BATH
15'-8" X 11'-4"

MASTER
SUITE
10' BOXED CEILING
15'-8" X 13'-8"

BRKFAST
RM.
11'-4" X 12'-0"

BEDROOM 2
11'-4" X 11'-0"

KITCHEN
11'-4" X 11'-2"

DW

REF
RG

GARAGE
12'-0" X 20'-0"

GARAGE
12'-0" X 20'-0"

KITCHEN
11'-4" X 11'-2"

DW

REF

BEDROOM 2
11'-4" X 11'-0"

BATH

GAS
FIREPLACE

GREAT RM.
10' BOXED CEILING
15'-8" X 16'-6"

GAS
FIREPLACE

GREAT RM.
10' BOXED CEILING
15'-8" X 16'-6"

BATH

BEDROOM 3 /
OFFICE
11'-4" X 12'-0"

COVERED
PORCH
16'-0" X 8'-0"
8" COLUMNS

COVERED
PORCH
16'-0" X 8'-0"
8" COLUMNS

BEDROOM 3 /
OFFICE
11'-4" X 12'-0"

PLAN DETAILS

- 2,840 total square feet of living area
- Living room is graced with a bay window and fireplace
- Bedroom includes a spacious walk-in closet
- Convenient laundry closet is located off hall
- First floor units have patios and second floor units have decks located off the dining area
- Each unit has 1 bedroom, 1 bath
- Basement foundation
- Fourplex has 710 square feet of living space per unit

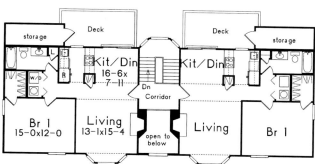

Second Floor
710 sq. ft. per unit

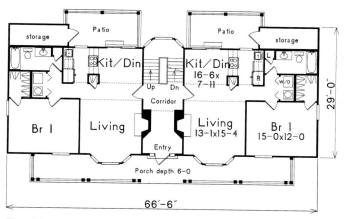

First Floor
710 sq. ft. per unit

PLAN NUMBER: 586-008D-0032
PRICE CODE: H

PLAN DETAILS

- 3,674 total square feet of living area
- Spacious second floor master bedroom has a large walk-in closet
- Kitchen has a snack counter which opens to the dining area and great room
- Each unit has 3 bedrooms, 2 1/2 baths, 2-car garage
- Basement foundation, drawings also include crawl space/slab foundation
- Duplex has 1,837 total square feet of living space per unit

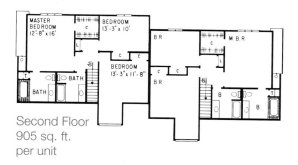

Second Floor
905 sq. ft.
per unit

MASTER BEDROOM 12'-8" x 16'
BEDROOM 13'-3" x 10'
BEDROOM 13'-3" x 11'-8"
BATH
BATH
B R
M B R
B R
B

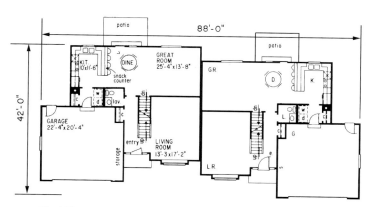

88'-0"

42'-0"

patio
patio

KIT 10'x11'-6"
DINE
snack counter
GREAT ROOM 25'-4"x13'-8"
GR
D
K

GARAGE 22'-4"x 20'-4"
lav.
entry
storage
LIVING ROOM 13'-3 x17'-2"
L R
G
LR
s

First Floor
932 sq. ft.
per unit

PLAN DETAILS

- 2,636 total square feet of living area
- Efficiently designed duplex provides space for each unit to have three bedrooms, including a deluxe master suite
- The spacious kitchen and charming nook unite with a laundry closet nearby
- The garage includes essential storage space and has access to the backyard
- Each unit has 3 bedrooms, 2 baths, 2-car garage
- Slab or crawl space foundation, please specify when ordering
- Duplex has 1,318 square feet of living area per unit

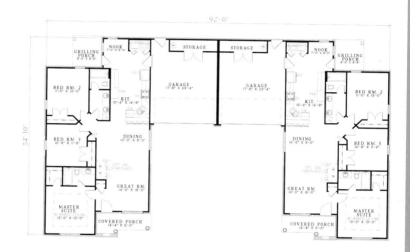

92'-0"

54'-10"

GRILLING PORCH
8'-0" X 8'-6"

NOOK
7'-0" X 8'-0"

STORAGE

STORAGE

NOOK
7'-0" X 8'-0"

GRILLING PORCH
8'-0" X 8'-6"

BED RM. 2
11'-0" X 13'-0"

KIT.
10'-4" X 14'-6"

GARAGE
17'-8" X 23'-4"

GARAGE
17'-8" X 23'-4"

KIT.
10'-4" X 14'-6"

BED RM. 2
11'-0" X 13'-0"

DINING
10'-0" X 9'-0"

DINING
10'-0" X 9'-0"

BED RM. 3
10'-8" X 11'-6"

BED RM. 3
10'-8" X 11'-6"

OPT. GAS FIREPLACE

OPT. GAS FIREPLACE

GREAT RM.
14'-0" X 16'-0"

GREAT RM.
14'-0" X 16'-0"

MASTER SUITE
13'-0" X 13'-0"

COVERED PORCH
14'-4" X 5'-0"

COVERED PORCH
14'-4" X 5'-0"

MASTER SUITE
13'-0" X 13'-0"

PLAN DETAILS

- 1,992 total square feet of living area
- Graciously designed ranch duplex with alluring openness
- Vaulted kitchen with accent on spaciousness features huge pantry, plenty of cabinets and convenient laundry room
- Master bedroom includes its own cozy bath and oversized walk-in closet
- Each unit has 2 bedrooms, 2 baths, 1-car garage
- Basement foundation
- Duplex has 996 square feet of living space per unit

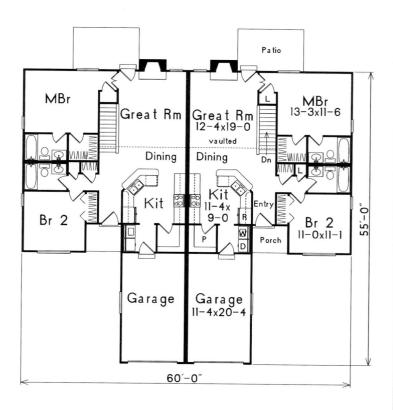

Patio

MBr

Great Rm | Great Rm
12-4x19-0
vaulted

MBr
13-3x11-6

L

Dining | Dining

Dn

Kit | Kit
11-4x
9-0

Br 2

Entry

R
W
D

Br 2
11-0x11-1

P

Porch

Garage | Garage
11-4x20-4

55'-0"

60'-0"

PLAN DETAILS

- 2,570 total square feet of living area
- U-shaped kitchen has all the conveniences
- First floor master bedroom is well located for privacy
- Two second floor bedrooms share a bath
- Each unit has 3 bedrooms, 2 baths, 2-car garage
- Crawl space or slab foundation, please specify when ordering
- Duplex has 1,285 square feet of living space per unit

Second Floor
374 sq. ft.
per unit

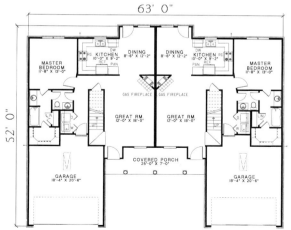

First Floor
911 sq. ft.
per unit

PLAN DETAILS

- 2,468 total square feet of living area
- Covered entrance welcomes guests and leads into the spacious living room
- Family room enjoys a fireplace and sliding doors to the rear patio
- A large laundry room includes space for a counter and sink
- Each unit has 2 bedrooms, 1 bath, 2-car garage
- Basement foundation
- Duplex has 1,234 square feet of living area per unit

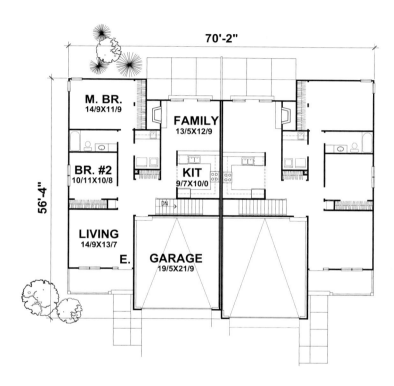

70'-2"

56'-4"

M. BR.
14/9X11/9

FAMILY
13/5X12/9

BR. #2
10/11X10/8

KIT
9/7X10/0

LIVING
14/9X13/7

DN

E.

GARAGE
19/5X21/9

PLAN DETAILS

- 2,166 total square feet of living area
- Energy efficient home with 2" x 6" exterior walls
- The central courtyard makes an impressive focal point
- The living room is open to the kitchen and dining area and includes a wood burning fireplace and sloped beamed ceiling
- A walk-in master closet, twin secondary bedroom closets, an entry closet and a built-in kitchen pantry provide abundant storage
- Each unit has 1,083 square feet of living area with 2 bedrooms and 2 baths
- Slab foundation

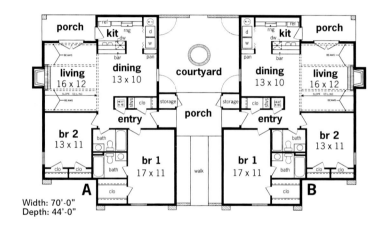

porch

kit
ref
rng
dw
bar
d
w
pan

living
16 x 12
BEAMS
SLOPE CEILING
BEAMS

dining
13 x 10

courtyard

dining
13 x 10

kit
ref
rng
dw
bar
d
w
pan

living
16 x 12
BEAMS
SLOPE CEILING
BEAMS

porch

HEAT
IN AIR
shvs
clo
storage

entry

porch

storage
clo
shvs
HEAT
IN AIR

entry

br 2
13 x 11

bath
bath

br 1
17 x 11

walk

br 1
17 x 11

bath
bath

br 2
13 x 11

clo   clo

clo

A

clo

clo

B

clo   clo

Width: 70'-0"
Depth: 44'-0"

PLAN DETAILS

- 3,666 total square feet of living area
- Inviting porch and foyer lead to the vaulted living room and dining balcony with atrium window wall
- Bedroom #2 doubles as a study with access to the deck through sliding glass doors
- Atrium opens to the large family room and third bedroom
- Each unit has 3 bedrooms, 2 baths, 2-car garage
- Walk-out basement foundation
- Duplex has 1,833 square feet of living space per unit

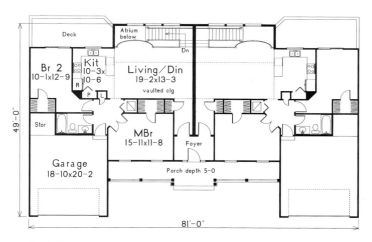

First Floor
1,073 sq. ft. per unit

Labels within first floor plan:
- Deck
- Atrium below
- Dn
- Br 2 10-1x12-9
- Kit 10-3x10-6
- Living/Din 19-2x13-3 vaulted clg
- R
- P L
- Stor
- MBr 15-11x11-8
- Foyer
- Garage 18-10x20-2
- Porch depth 5-0
- 49'-0"
- 81'-0"

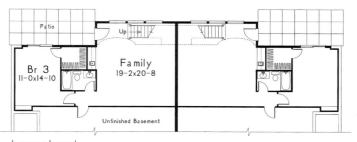

Lower Level
760 sq. ft. per unit

Labels within lower level plan:
- Patio
- Up
- Br 3 11-0x14-10
- Family 19-2x20-8
- Unfinished Basement

PLAN DETAILS

- 3,648 total square feet of living area
- Large kitchen adjacent to living room
- Handy linen closet in hallway
- Spacious living area with easy access to a patio or balcony
- Centrally located laundry closet for stackable washer and dryer
- Each unit has 2 bedrooms, 1 bath
- Crawl space/slab foundation
- Fourplex has 912 square feet of living space per unit

Second Floor
912 sq. ft. per unit

BEDROOM
11'-7"x10'-5"

c

BEDROOM
12'x12'

B R

c

B R

c

h
w

BATH

B.

c

h
w

W/d

W/d

KITCHEN
11'-7"x10'

K

entry

c c

e

porch

dn

LIVING
ROOM
19'-3"x12'-9"

L R

balcony

balcony

56'-0"

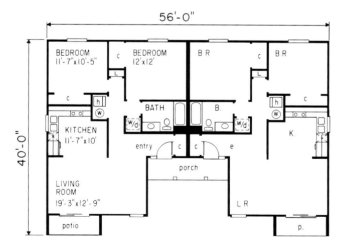

BEDROOM
11'-7"x10'-5"

c

BEDROOM
12'x12'

B R

c

B R

c

h
w

BATH

B.

c

h
w

40'-0"

W/d

W/d

KITCHEN
11'-7"x10'

K

entry

c c

e

porch

LIVING
ROOM
19'-3"x12'-9"

L R

patio

p.

First Floor
912 sq. ft. per unit

PLAN DETAILS

- 3,620 total square feet of living area
- 9' ceilings throughout the first floor
- Impressive master suite has a private bath, walk-in closet and easy access to the laundry room
- Each unit has 3 bedrooms, 2 1/2 baths, 2-car garage
- Crawl space or slab foundation, please specify when ordering
- Duplex has 1,810 square feet of living space per unit

Second Floor
441 sq. ft.
per unit

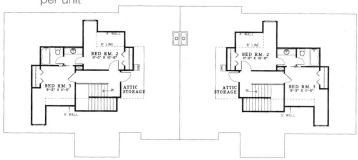

First Floor
1,369 sq. ft.
per unit

PLAN DETAILS

- 4,131 total square feet of living area
- Unit A has 3 bedrooms, 2 baths, 2-car garage
- Unit B has 3 bedrooms, 2 1/2 baths, 2-car garage
- Unit A has a luxurious master bedroom with double walk-in closets and a private bath with step-up tub, separate shower and double vanity
- Unit B features a master suite on the first floor and all bedrooms have walk-in closets
- Slab foundation

Unit B
Second Floor
642 sq. ft.

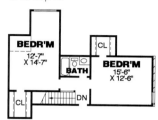

BEDR'M
12'-7" X 14'-7"

BATH

CL

BEDR'M
15'-6" X 12'-6"

CL

DN

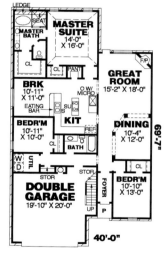

LEDGE

SEAT

MASTER BATH

CL

MASTER SUITE
14'-0" X 16'-0"

CL PANT

F/P

BRK
10'-11" X 11'-0"

O W/ MICRO

GREAT ROOM
15'-2" X 18'-0"

EATING BAR

SU S

KIT

BEDR'M
10'-11" X 10'-0"

REF

CL

BATH

DINING
10'-4" X 12'-0"

69'-7"

W D

UTIL

STOR

STOR

FOYER

CL

BEDR'M
10'-10" X 13'-0"

DOUBLE GARAGE
19'-10" X 20'-0"

UP

P

40'-0"

Unit A
First Floor
1,936 sq. ft.

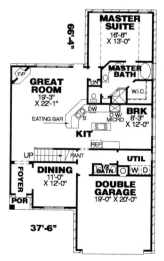

66'-4"

MASTER SUITE
16'-8" X 13'-0"

MASTER BATH

W.I.C.

F/P

GREAT ROOM
19'-3" X 22'-1"

LIN

DW

O W/ MICRO

BRK
8'-3" X 12'-0"

EATING BAR

S

KIT

REF

PANT

UP

DINING
11'-0" X 12'-0"

1/2 BATH

O W D

UTIL

DOUBLE GARAGE
19'-0" X 20'-0"

FOYER

POR

37'-6"

Unit B
First Floor
1,553 sq. ft.

261

PLAN DETAILS

- 2,758 total square feet of living area
- A 10' ceiling in the foyer provides a grand first impression and leads into the massive great room
- The cheerful breakfast room and luxurious master suite both enjoy access onto the covered porch
- The garage conveniently enters the home through the large laundry room with pantry
- Each unit has 3 bedrooms, 2 baths, 2-car garage
- Slab or crawl space foundation, please specify when ordering
- Duplex has 1,379 square feet of living area per unit

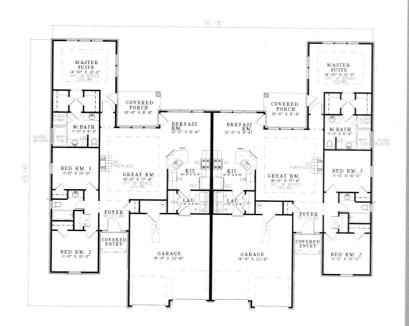

76'-8"

65'-6"

MASTER SUITE
14'-10" X 12'-0"
OPT. @ BOXED CEILING

COVERED PORCH
10'-6" X 8'-8"

BRKFAST RM.
12'-0" X 9'-4"

M.BATH
11'-0" X 8'-4"

GLASS SHWR

GLASS BLOCKS

WHP TUB

BED RM. 3
11'-0" X 10'-0"

GAS FIREPLACE

GREAT RM.
16'-0" X 17'-4"
OPT. @ BOXED CEILING

KIT.
10'-0" X 9'-4"

RG

DW

REF

LAU.
7'-4" X 8'-4"

D

W

PAN

FOYER
9' CEILING

COVERED ENTRY

BED RM. 2
11'-0" X 10'-0"

GARAGE
19'-4" X 22'-6"

BRKFAST RM.
12'-0" X 9'-4"

KIT.
10'-0" X 9'-4"

RG

DW

REF

LAU.
7'-4" X 8'-4"

D

W

PAN

GREAT RM.
16'-0" X 17'-4"
OPT. @ BOXED CEILING

GAS FIREPLACE

COVERED PORCH
10'-6" X 8'-8"

MASTER SUITE
14'-10" X 12'-0"
OPT. @ BOXED CEILING

M.BATH
11'-0" X 8'-4"

GLASS SHWR

LIN

WHP TUB

GLASS BLOCKS

BED RM. 3
11'-0" X 10'-0"

FOYER
9' CEILING

COVERED ENTRY

BED RM. 2
11'-0" X 10'-0"

GARAGE
19'-4" X 22'-6"

PLAN DETAILS

- 4,740 total square feet of living area
- Elegant four-plex designed for spacious living
- Unit B has 1,198 square feet of living area with 641 square feet on the first floor and 557 square feet on the second floor
- Unit A has 1,172 square feet of living area with 628 square feet on the first floor and 544 square feet on the second floor
- Each unit has 3 bedrooms, 1 1/2 baths
- Basement foundation

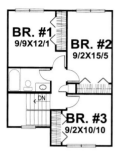

Unit A Second Floor
544 sq. ft.

BR. #1
9/9X12/1

BR. #2
9/2X15/5

BR. #3
9/2X10/10

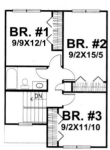

Unit B Second Floor
557 sq. ft.

BR. #1
9/9X12/1

BR. #2
9/2X15/5

BR. #3
9/2X11/10

22'-0"

31'-4"

KIT
8/9X9/1

DINING
12/5X9/0

LIVING
12/5X20/0

Unit A First Floor
628 sq. ft.

22'-0"

32'-4"

KIT
8/9X9/1

DINING
12/5X9/0

LIVING
12/5X21/0

Unit B First Floor
641 sq. ft.

265

PLAN DETAILS

- 2,445 total square feet of living area
- 10' ceiling in the great room along with transoms flanking the fireplace create a breathtaking atmosphere
- Kitchen includes a convenient snack bar overlooking the sunny breakfast room
- Master bedroom has a box-bay window, private bath and an enormous walk-in closet
- Each unit has 2 bedrooms, 2 baths, 2-car garage
- Basement foundation

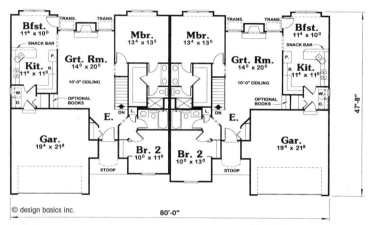

Bfst.
11^4 x 10^0

SNACK BAR

Kit.
11^4 x 11^0

Grt. Rm.
14^0 x 20^0

10'-0" CEILING

OPTIONAL BOOKS

Gar.
19^4 x 21^8

E.

DN

STOOP

TRANS. TRANS.

Mbr.
13^4 x 13^0

Mbr.
13^4 x 13^0

Br. 2
10^0 x 11^0

Br. 2
10^0 x 13^0

TRANS. TRANS.

Bfst.
11^4 x 10^0

SNACK BAR

Grt. Rm.
14^0 x 20^0

10'-0" CEILING

OPTIONAL BOOKS

Kit.
11^4 x 11^0

E.

DN

STOOP

Gar.
19^4 x 21^8

47'-8"

© design basics inc.

80'-0"

Unit A
1,212 sq. ft.

Unit B
1,233 sq. ft.

PLAN DETAILS

- 3,502 total square feet of living area
- Two-story entry has an elegant staircase that leads to the living room with a fireplace
- Breakfast room enjoys a bay window, sliding glass doors to outdoor balcony and a pass-through to the kitchen
- A lower level laundry area is provided in each unit
- Each unit has 3 bedrooms, 2 1/2 baths, 2-car drive under garage
- Walk-out basement foundation
- Duplex has 1,751 square feet of living space per unit including 252 square feet on the lower level

Second Floor
707 sq. ft. per unit

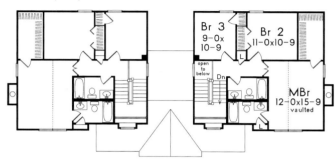

Br 3
9-0x
10-9

Br 2
11-0x10-9

open
to
below

Dn

MBr
12-0x15-9
vaulted

68'-0"

Balcony

27'-6"

Dining
11-0x11-0

Kit
10-0x
10-8

Brk
9-0x
11-0

Entry

Up   Dn

Living
15-2x15-10

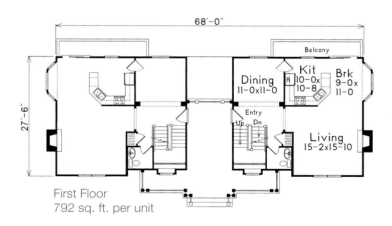

First Floor
792 sq. ft. per unit

PLAN DETAILS

- 3,066 total square feet of living area
- Master bedroom has a private bath, sitting area, walk-in closet and access outdoors
- Kitchen has a vaulted ceiling and a snack counter that overlooks the living room
- Living room enjoys a fireplace, vaulted ceiling and access to deck
- Each unit has 3 bedrooms, 2 baths, 2-car garage
- Basement foundation
- Duplex has 1,533 square feet of living space per unit

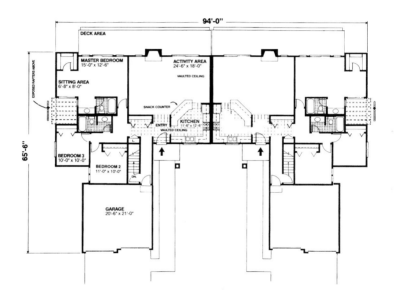

94'-0"

65'-6"

DECK AREA

EXPOSED RAFTERS ABOVE

MASTER BEDROOM
15'-0" x 12'-6"

ACTIVITY AREA
24'-6" x 18'-0"

VAULTED CEILING

SITTING AREA
6'-8" x 8'-0"

SNACK COUNTER

ENTRY

KITCHEN
11'-6" x 12'-6"

VAULTED CEILING

BEDROOM 3
10'-0" x 10'-0"

BEDROOM 2
11'-0" x 10'-0"

DN.

GARAGE
20'-6" x 21'-0"

PLAN DETAILS

- 4,240 total square feet of living area
- Kitchen, brightened by a large bay window, accesses patio on the first floor units and deck on the second floor units
- Corner fireplace provides warmth and charm
- Bedrooms are separated from living areas for privacy
- Laundry is located off hall for accessibility
- Each unit has 3 bedrooms, 2 baths, 1-car garage
- Basement foundation
- Fourplex has 1,060 square feet of living space per unit

Second Floor
1,060 sq. ft. per unit

Deck | Deck

Br 2 | Br 3 | Kit | Kit 12-6x12-3 | Br 3 9-0x 10-0 | Br 2 11-0x10-0

R | P

MBr | Living | Balcony open to below | Living 12-6x18-0 | W D | L | MBr 14-0x12-0

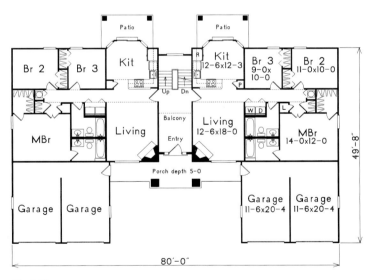

First Floor
1,060 sq. ft. per unit

Patio | Patio

Br 2 | Br 3 | Kit | Kit 12-6x12-3 | Br 3 9-0x 10-0 | Br 2 11-0x10-0

R | Up Dn | P

MBr | Living | Balcony | Entry | Living 12-6x18-0 | W D | L | MBr 14-0x12-0

Porch depth 5-0

Garage | Garage | Garage 11-6x20-4 | Garage 11-6x20-4

80'-0"

49'-8"

PLAN NUMBER: 586-025D-0064

PRICE CODE: H

PLAN DETAILS

- 6,002 total square feet of living area
- All master baths have step-up tubs, separate showers, double vanities and walk-in closets
- Unit C has 2 bedrooms, 2 baths, 2-car garage
- Unit D has 3 bedrooms, 2 1/2 baths, 2-car garage
- Unit E has 3 bedrooms, 2 baths, 2-car garage
- Slab foundation

Unit E
1,939 sq. ft.

GREAT ROOM
19'-0" X 15'-0"
DECORATIVE CEILING

EATING BAR

BEDR'M
12'-0" X 11'-0"
CL

BEDR'M
11'-8" X 11'-0"

KIT
BRK
O.W.
MICRO
BATH
CL

DINING
12'-6" X 11'-6"

PANT

MASTER BATH
GALLERY

CL

UTIL
W
D

UP

MASTER SUITE
14'-1" X 16'-0"

ENTRY

DOUBLE GARAGE

POR

42'-8"

66'-0"

Unit D
Second Floor
1,127 sq. ft.

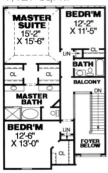

MASTER SUITE
15'-2" X 15'-6"

BEDR'M
12'-2" X 11'-5"

LIN
CL

BATH

CL
CL

BALCONY

MASTER BATH

DN

BEDR'M
12'-6" X 13'-0"

LIN

CL

FOYER BELOW

Unit C
1,972 sq. ft.

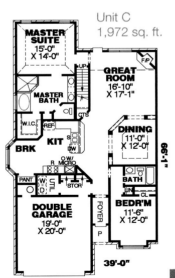

MASTER SUITE
15'-0" X 14'-0"

UP

GREAT ROOM
16'-10" X 17'-1"

F.P.

MASTER BATH

CTS

W.I.C.
REF
S

DINING
11'-0" X 12'-0"

KIT
O.W.
MICRO
R.

BRK

PANT
W
D
UTIL
STOR

LIN

BATH

CL

DOUBLE GARAGE
19'-0" X 20'-0"

FOYER

BEDR'M
11'-6" X 12'-0"

P

66'-1"

39'-0"

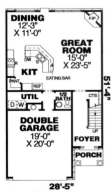

DINING
12'-3" X 11'-0"

F.P.

GREAT ROOM
15'-0" X 23'-5"

DW

KIT
EATING BAR

PANT
REF

UTIL
D W

1/2 **BATH**

CTS

DOUBLE GARAGE
19'-0" X 20'-0"

FOYER

UP

PORCH

28'-5"

51'-4"

Unit D
First Floor
964 sq. ft.

PLAN DETAILS

- 3,308 total square feet of living area
- Duplex features an elegant brick facade with stylish windows
- Both units feature a large kitchen that includes a pantry and snack bar and opens to the dining/hearth room
- A lavish master suite and two secondary bedrooms make this an ideal family home
- Each unit has 3 bedrooms, 2 baths, 2-car garage
- Slab or crawl space foundation, please specify when ordering
- Duplex has 1,654 square feet of living area per unit

98'-0"

58'-6"

GLASS BLOCK

M. BATH

COVERED PORCH
15'-4" X 7'-0"

BED RM. 3
12'-8" X 10'-10"

BED RM. 3
12'-8" X 10'-10"

COVERED PORCH
15'-4" X 7'-0"

GLASS BLOCK

M. BATH

WHP TUB

WHP TUB

MASTER SUITE
10' BOXED CEILING
14'-0" X 13'-0"

DINING RM. /
HEARTH RM.
15'-4" X 12'-0"

BATH

BATH

DINING RM. /
HEARTH RM.
15'-4" X 12'-0"

MASTER SUITE
10' BOXED CEILING
14'-0" X 13'-0"

LAU.
6'-10" X 5'-6"

LAU.
6'-10" X 5'-6"

STRG.
7'-8" X 5'-6"

KITCHEN
13'-0" X 13'-0"

BED RM. 2
12'-8" X 12'-4"

BED RM. 2
12'-8" X 12'-4"

KITCHEN
13'-0" X 13'-0"

STRG.
7'-8" X 5'-6"

REF.

REF.

GARAGE
19'-8" X 20'-0"

FOYER

SLOPED CEILING

SLOPED CEILING

FOYER

GARAGE
19'-8" X 20'-0"

PRCH

GREAT RM.
11' FLAT CEILING
15'-4" X 18'-0"

GREAT RM.
11' FLAT CEILING
15'-4" X 18'-0"

PRCH

MEDIA CENTER

MEDIA CENTER

277

PLAN DETAILS

- 896 total square feet of living area
- Small cabin duplex is well suited for rental property or permanent residence
- Compact, yet convenient floor plan
- Well organized for economical construction
- 1 bedroom, 1 bath
- Slab foundation
- Duplex has 448 square feet of living space per unit

Rear View

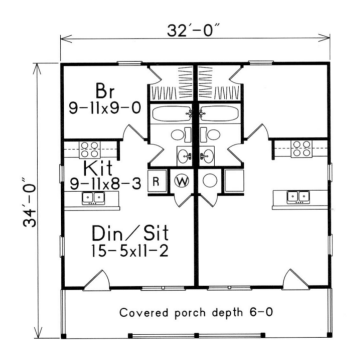

32´-0"

34´-0"

Br
9-11x9-0

Kit
9-11x8-3

R W

Din/Sit
15-5x11-2

Covered porch depth 6-0

PLAN DETAILS

- 2,953 total square feet of living area
- The foyer spills into the expansive great room and captures a grand view of the backyard from the wall of windows
- This duplex design includes conveniences such as a large laundry room and storage closet located in the garage
- Each unit has 3 bedrooms, 2 baths, 2-car garage
- Slab or crawl space foundation, please specify when ordering
- Unit A has 1,481 square feet of living area and Unit B has 1,472 square feet of living area

Unit A
1,481 sq. ft.

Unit B
1,472 sq. ft.

PLAN DETAILS

- 2,901 total square feet of living area
- Three first floor units have access to their own balcony while the two lower level units each enjoy private patios
- Each unit has 1 bedroom, 1 bath
- Walk-out basement foundation
- Units A and C each have 600 square feet of living area, Unit B has 517 square feet of living area and Units D and E each have 592 square feet of living area
- Fiveplex has 1,717 square feet of living area on the first floor and 1,184 square feet of living area on the lower level

First Floor

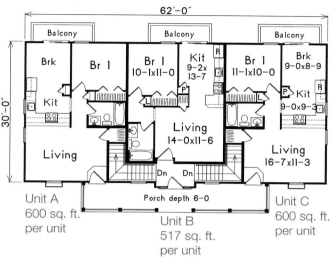

62'-0"

30'-0"

| Balcony | Balcony | Balcony |

Brk
Br 1
Br 1
10-1x11-0
Kit
9-2x
13-7
Br 1
11-1x10-0
Brk
9-0x8-9

Kit

Living
14-0x11-6

Living

Kit
9-0x9-3

Living
16-7x11-3

Dn Dn

Porch depth 6-0

Unit A
600 sq. ft.
per unit

Unit B
517 sq. ft.
per unit

Unit C
600 sq. ft.
per unit

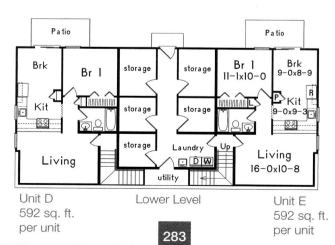

| Patio | | Patio |

Brk
Br 1
storage
storage
Br 1
11-1x10-0
Brk
9-0x8-9

Kit
storage
storage
Kit
9-0x9-3

storage
Laundry
Up

Living
utility
Living
16-0x10-8

Unit D
592 sq. ft.
per unit

Lower Level

Unit E
592 sq. ft.
per unit

PLAN DETAILS

- 3,636 total square feet of living area
- Bayed breakfast room is centrally located between the great room and kitchen
- Two-story foyer adds a dramatic feel with plant shelves above
- Great room has fireplace and wall of windows creating a cheerful atmosphere
- Each unit has 3 bedrooms, 2 1/2 baths, 2-car garage
- Basement foundation
- Duplex has 1,818 square feet of living space per unit

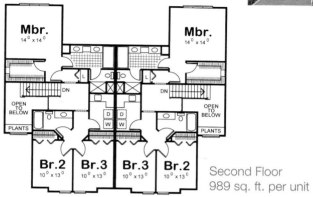

Mbr.
14⁰ x 14⁰

Mbr.
14⁰ x 14⁰

DN

DN

OPEN
TO
BELOW

OPEN
TO
BELOW

PLANTS

PLANTS

Br.2
10⁰ x 13⁰

Br.3
10⁰ x 13⁰

Br.3
10⁰ x 13⁰

Br.2
10⁰ x 13⁰

Second Floor
989 sq. ft. per unit

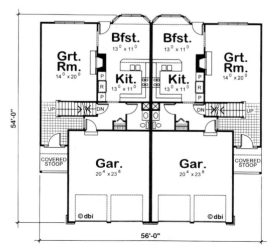

Bfst.
13⁰ x 11⁰

Bfst.
13⁰ x 11⁰

**Grt.
Rm.**
14⁰ x 20⁰

**Grt.
Rm.**
14⁰ x 20⁰

Kit.
13⁰ x 11⁰

Kit.
13⁰ x 11⁰

UP

DN

DN

UP

COVERED
STOOP

COVERED
STOOP

Gar.
20⁴ x 23⁸

Gar.
20⁴ x 23⁸

©dbi

©dbi

54'-0"

56'-0"

First Floor
829 sq. ft. per unit

PLAN NUMBER: 586-055D-0062

PRICE CODE: F

PLAN DETAILS

- 2,502 total square feet of living area
- Decorative columns separate the dining area from the great room
- All bedrooms are located on the second floor for privacy
- Each unit has 3 bedrooms, 2 1/2 baths, 1-car garage
- Crawl space or slab foundation, please specify when ordering
- Duplex has 1,251 square feet of living space per unit

Second Floor
642 sq. ft. per unit

BEDROOM 2
8'-10" X 10'-4"

M.BATH

MBEDRM.
10'-8" X 15'-0"

MBEDRM.
10'-8" X 15'-0"

M.BATH

BEDROOM 2
8'-10" X 10'-4"

LIN

DN

LIN

DN

BATH

BATH

BEDROOM 3
12'-4" X 10'-0"

BEDROOM 3
12'-4" X 10'-0"

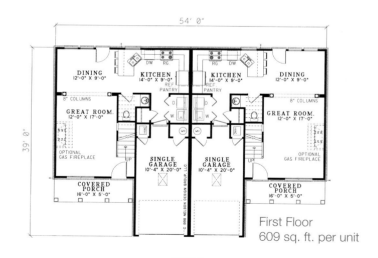

54' 0"

39' 0"

DINING
12'-0" X 9'-0"

KITCHEN
14'-0" X 9'-0"

DW   RG

RG   DW

KITCHEN
14'-0" X 9'-0"

DINING
12'-0" X 9'-0"

REF.
PANTRY

REF.
PANTRY

8" COLUMNS

8" COLUMNS

GREAT ROOM.
12'-0" X 17'-0"

GREAT ROOM.
12'-0" X 17'-0"

W

W

OPTIONAL
GAS FIREPLACE

OPTIONAL
GAS FIREPLACE

UP

UP

SINGLE
GARAGE
10'-4" X 20'-0"

SINGLE
GARAGE
10'-4" X 20'-0"

COVERED
PORCH
16'-0" X 5'-0"

COVERED
PORCH
16'-0" X 5'-0"

© 1998 NELSON DESIGN GROUP, LLC

First Floor
609 sq. ft. per unit

PLAN DETAILS

- 2,436 total square feet of living area
- Master bedroom has a private bath with double vanities and a large walk-in closet
- Kitchen with snack bar overlooks breakfast room
- Great room has a cheerful wall of windows brightening the interior
- Each unit has 2 bedrooms, 2 baths, 2-car garage
- Basement foundation
- Duplex has 1,218 square feet of living space per unit

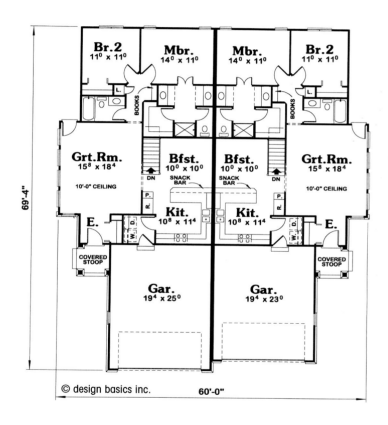

Br. 2
11⁰ x 11⁰

Mbr.
14⁰ x 11⁰

Mbr.
14⁰ x 11⁰

Br. 2
11⁰ x 11⁰

L.

BOOKS

BOOKS

L.

Grt. Rm.
15⁸ x 18⁴

10'-0" CEILING

Bfst.
10⁰ x 10⁰

DN

SNACK
BAR

Bfst.
10⁰ x 10⁰

SNACK
BAR

DN

Grt. Rm.
15⁸ x 18⁴

10'-0" CEILING

E.

P.

R.

Kit.
10⁸ x 11⁴

Kit.
10⁸ x 11⁴

R.

P.

E.

W. D.

W. D.

COVERED
STOOP

COVERED
STOOP

Gar.
19⁴ x 25⁰

Gar.
19⁴ x 23⁰

69'-4"

© design basics inc.

60'-0"

PLAN DETAILS

- 3,050 total square feet of living area
- A beautiful boxed ceiling in the great room adds an elegant feel
- Convenient and functional covered porch and grilling porch extend the living areas outdoors
- Separate master suite creates a private feel
- Each unit has 3 bedrooms, 2 baths, 2-car garage
- Crawl space or slab foundation, please specify when ordering
- Duplex has 1,525 square feet of living space per unit

103'-0"

49'-10"

GRILLING PORCH
10'-6" X 9'-2"

COVERED PORCH
13'-2" X 9'-2"

6" BOXED COLUMNS

MASTER SUITE
16'-8" X 13'-0"

9' BOXED CEILING

MASTER SUITE
16'-8" X 13'-0"

9' BOXED CEILING

COVERED PORCH
13'-2" X 9'-2"

6" BOXED COLUMNS

GRILLING PORCH
10'-6" X 9'-2"

DINING
11'-0" X 9'-6"

KITCHEN
16'-2" X 13'-4"

BATH

M. BATH
16'-0" X 9'-6"

GREAT ROOM
19'-0" X 19'-8"

9' BOXED CEILING

M. BATH
16'-0" X 9'-6"

GREAT ROOM
19'-0" X 19'-8"

9' BOXED CEILING

DINING
11'-0" X 9'-6"

KITCHEN
16'-2" X 13'-4"

BATH

LAU
9'-4" X 6'-4"

LAU
9'-4" X 6'-4"

BEDROOM 2
10'-2" X 10'-8"

BEDROOM 3 / STUDY
10'-0" X 10'-8"

FOYER

GARAGE
20'-10" X 20'-0"

GARAGE
20'-10" X 20'-0"

FOYER

BEDROOM 3 / STUDY
10'-0" X 10'-8"

BEDROOM 2
10'-2" X 10'-8"

COVERED PORCH
16'-6" X 6'-0"

10" BOXED COLUMNS

COVERED PORCH
16'-6" X 6'-0"

8" BOXED COLUMN

PLAN NUMBER: 586-058D-0018

PRICE CODE: C

PLAN DETAILS

- 1,352 total square feet of living area
- See-through fireplace from the living room into the bedroom makes a lasting impression
- Covered front porch is perfect for relaxing evenings
- Galley-style kitchen is compact but well organized for efficiency
- Each unit has 1 bedroom, 1 bath
- Slab foundation
- Duplex has 676 square feet of living space per unit

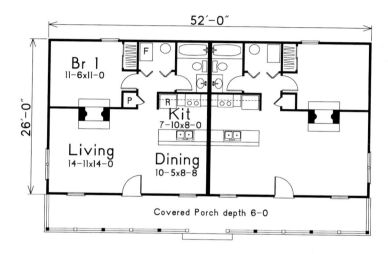

52'-0"

26'-0"

Br 1
11-6x11-0

F

Kit
7-10x8-0

P

R

Living
14-11x14-0

Dining
10-5x8-8

Covered Porch depth 6-0

Rear View

293

PLAN DETAILS

- 1,076 total square feet of living area
- A country porch for quiet times leads to a living room with fireplace, dining area and efficient kitchenette
- The bedroom offers a double-door entry, walk-in closet and a bath with linen closet
- Spacious and private screen porch is steps away from the dining area through sliding doors
- Each unit has 1 bedroom, 1 bath
- Crawl space foundation, drawings also include slab foundation
- Duplex has 538 square feet of living space per unit

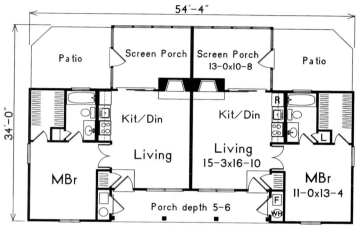

54'-4"

34'-0"

Patio

Screen Porch

Screen Porch
13-0x10-8

Patio

Kit/Din

Kit/Din

R

Living

Living
15-3x16-10

MBr

MBr
11-0x13-4

F
WH

Porch depth 5-6

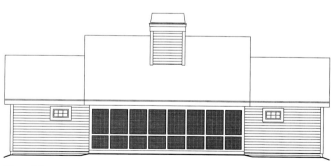

Rear View

PLAN DETAILS

- 1,536 total square feet of living area
- Living room joins the kitchen/dining area for an open atmosphere
- L-shaped kitchen with outdoor access and convenient laundry area
- Linen and coat closet
- Welcoming front porch
- Each unit has 2 bedrooms, 1 bath
- Crawl space foundation, drawings also include slab foundation
- Duplex has 768 total square feet of living space per unit

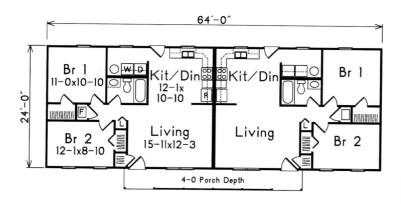

64'-0"

24'-0"

Br 1
11-0x10-10

W·D

Kit/Din
12-1x
10-10

Kit/Din

Br 1

F

Br 2
12-1x8-10

Living
15-11x12-3

Living

Br 2

4-0 Porch Depth

Rear View

PLAN DETAILS

- 1,636 total square feet of living area
- Large windows decorate the facade and flood the interior with warm, natural light
- The massive living room is open to the kitchen creating a spacious living area
- The kitchen enjoys access to the rear porch where an essential storage closet is located
- Each unit has 2 bedrooms, 1 bath
- Slab or crawl space foundation, please specify when ordering
- Duplex has 818 square feet of living area per unit

MULTI-FAMILY HOME

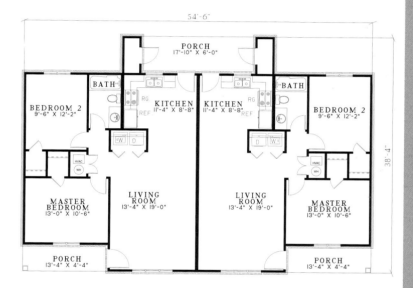

54'-6"

PORCH
17'-10" X 6'-0"

BATH

BEDROOM 2
9'-6" X 12'-2"

KITCHEN
11'-4" X 8'-8"

KITCHEN
11'-4" X 8'-8"

BATH

BEDROOM 2
9'-6" X 12'-2"

RG
REF

RG
REF

W D

D W

HVAC
WH

HVAC
WH

LIVING
ROOM
13'-4" X 19'-0"

LIVING
ROOM
13'-4" X 19'-0"

MASTER
BEDROOM
13'-0" X 10'-6"

MASTER
BEDROOM
13'-0" X 10'-6"

38'-4"

PORCH
13'-4" X 4'-4"

PORCH
13'-4" X 4'-4"

PLAN DETAILS

- 2,986 total square feet of living area
- Vaulted great room, kitchen and two balconies define architectural drama
- First floor master bedroom has a lavish bath and double walk-in closets
- Impressive second floor features two large bedrooms, spacious closets, hall bath and balcony overlook
- Each unit has 3 bedrooms, 2 1/2 baths, 2-car garage
- Basement foundation
- Duplex has 1,493 square feet of living space per unit

Second Floor
533 sq. ft.
per unit

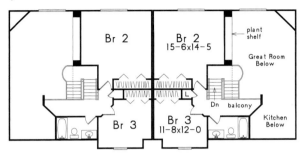

plant shelf

Br 2

Br 2
15-6x14-5

Great Room Below

Dn   balcony

Br 3

Br 3
11-8x12-0

Kitchen Below

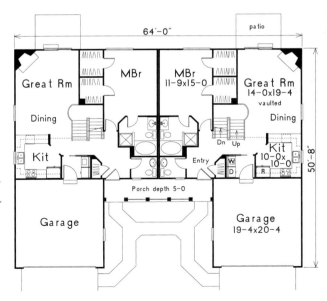

64'-0"

patio

Great Rm

MBr

MBr
11-9x15-0

Great Rm
14-0x19-4
vaulted

Dining

Dining

Kit

Dn   Up

Entry

Kit
10-0x
10-0

W
D

R

First Floor
960 sq. ft.
per unit

Porch depth 5-0

Garage

Garage
19-4x20-4

50'-8"

PLAN DETAILS

- 4,023 total square feet of living area
- Family room has fireplace for coziness and access outdoors on a covered porch
- Laundry closet is located on the second floor near bedrooms for convenience
- Master bedroom has private bath with double vanity, large walk-in closet and a sunny sitting area
- Each unit has 2 bedrooms, 2 1/2 baths, 1-car drive under garage
- Basement foundation
- Triplex has 1,341 square feet of living space per unit

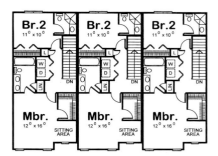

Br.2
11⁰ x 10⁰

Br.2
11⁰ x 10⁰

Br.2
11⁰ x 10⁰

Mbr.
12⁰ x 16⁰
SITTING AREA

Mbr.
12⁰ x 16⁰
SITTING AREA

Mbr.
12⁰ x 16⁰
SITTING AREA

Second Floor
657 sq. ft. per unit

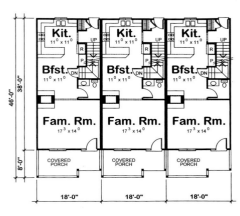

Kit.
11⁰ x 11⁰

Kit.
11⁰ x 11⁰

Kit.
11⁰ x 11⁰

Bfst.
11⁰ x 11⁰

Bfst.
11⁰ x 11⁰

Bfst.
11⁰ x 11⁰

Fam. Rm.
17³ x 14⁰

Fam. Rm.
17³ x 14⁰

Fam. Rm.
17³ x 14⁰

COVERED PORCH

COVERED PORCH

COVERED PORCH

46'-0"   38'-0"   8'-0"

18'-0"   18'-0"   18'-0"

First Floor
684 sq. ft.
per unit

Bsmt.
12¹⁰ x 13⁰

Bsmt.
12¹⁰ x 13⁰

Bsmt.
12¹⁰ x 13⁰

Gar.
16⁸ x 23²

Gar.
16⁸ x 23²

Gar.
16⁸ x 23²

©dbi   ©dbi   ©dbi

Lower Level

303

PLAN NUMBER: 586-055D-0073

PRICE CODE: G

PLAN DETAILS

- 2,854 total square feet of living area
- 9' ceilings throughout this duplex
- The great room enjoys a 10' box ceiling and a cozy fireplace
- Bedroom #3 could easily be converted to a study
- Kitchen features an eat-in bar which opens to the hearth room
- Each unit has 3 bedrooms, 2 baths, 1-car garage
- Crawl space or slab foundation, please specify when ordering
- Duplex has 1,427 square feet of living space per unit

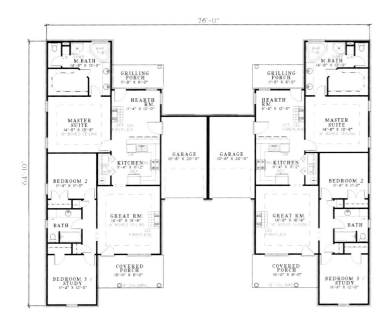

76'-0"

64'-10"

M.BATH
14'-8" X 13'-0"

GRILLING
PORCH
11'-8" X 6'-0"

HEARTH
RM.
11'-4" X 12'-0"

OPT. GAS
FIREPLACE

MASTER
SUITE
14'-8" X 13'-8"
10' BOXED CEILING

GARAGE
10'-8" X 20'-0"

KITCHEN
11'-4" X 11'-2"
REF.

BEDROOM 2
11'-4" X 11'-0"

GREAT RM.
14'-8" X 16'-6"
10' BOXED CEILING

GAS
FIREPLACE

BATH

COVERED
PORCH
15'-0" X 8'-0"

BEDROOM 3 /
STUDY
11'-4" X 12'-0"

8" COLUMNS

M.BATH
14'-8" X 13'-0"

GRILLING
PORCH
11'-8" X 6'-0"

HEARTH
RM.
11'-4" X 12'-0"

OPT. GAS
FIREPLACE

MASTER
SUITE
14'-8" X 13'-8"
10' BOXED CEILING

GARAGE
10'-8" X 20'-0"

KITCHEN
11'-4" X 11'-2"
REF.

BEDROOM 2
11'-4" X 11'-0"

GREAT RM.
14'-8" X 16'-6"
10' BOXED CEILING

GAS
FIREPLACE

BATH

COVERED
PORCH
15'-0" X 8'-0"

BEDROOM 3 /
STUDY
11'-4" X 12'-0"

8" COLUMNS

PLAN DETAILS

- 2,830 total square feet of living area
- Great room, master bedroom and dining room access covered porch
- Master bedroom features a double-door entry, walk-in closet and private bath with shower
- Great room has a fireplace and wet bar
- Laundry room has plenty of workspace
- Each unit has 2 bedrooms, 2 baths, 2-car garage
- Basement foundation
- Duplex has 1,415 square feet of living space per unit

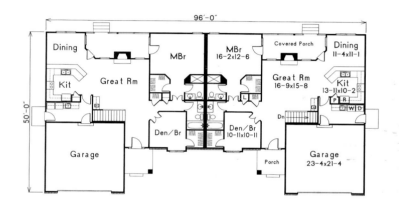

96'-0"

50'-0"

Dining

MBr

Great Rm

Kit

MBr
16-2x12-6

Covered Porch

Great Rm
16-9x15-8

Dining
11-4x11-1

Kit
13-11x10-2

P R

W D

Garage

Den/Br

Den/Br
10-11x10-11

Dn

Garage
23-4x21-4

Porch

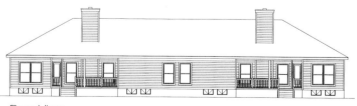

Rear View

PLAN DETAILS

- 2,408 total square feet of living area
- The large great room offers a fireplace and dining area with view of the patio
- Each unit enjoys its own private garage, front porch and rear patio
- The second floor bedrooms are large in size and feature spacious walk-in closets
- Each unit has 2 bedrooms, 1 1/2 baths, 1-car garage
- Basement foundation
- Duplex has 1,204 square feet of living space per unit

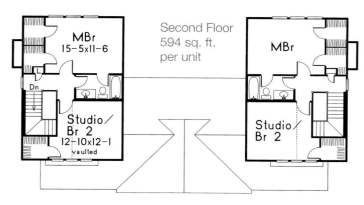

Second Floor
594 sq. ft.
per unit

MBr
15-5x11-6

MBr

Dn

**Studio/
Br 2**
12-10x12-1
vaulted

**Studio/
Br 2**

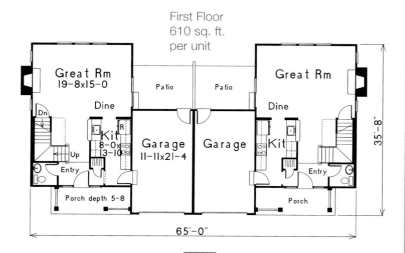

First Floor
610 sq. ft.
per unit

Great Rm
19-8x15-0

Great Rm

Dine

Dine

Patio

Patio

Kit
8-0x
13-10

R

Garage
11-11x21-4

Garage

Kit

Dn

Up

Entry

Entry

Porch depth 5-8

Porch

35'-8"

65'-0"

PLAN DETAILS

- 2,774 total square feet of living area
- 9' ceilings throughout home
- Kitchen has snack bar open to dining room
- Garage includes golf cart storage
- Windows across the great room and dining room rear walls create a cheerful atmosphere
- Each unit has 2 bedrooms, 2 baths, 2-car garage
- Crawl space or slab foundation, please specify when ordering
- Duplex has 1,387 square feet of living space per unit

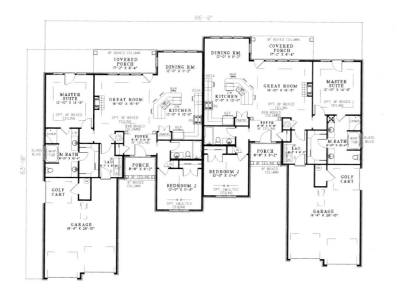

86'-0"

63'-10"

MASTER SUITE
12'-10" X 14'-8"

OPT. 10' BOXED CEILING

COVERED PORCH
17'-2" X 6'-4"

10' BOXED COLUMN

DINING RM.
12'-0" X 11'-2"

GREAT ROOM
16'-10" X 15'-5"

OPT. 10' BOXED CEILING

8X8 BOXED COLUMNS

KITCHEN
12'-0" X 13'-0"

DW

BAR

REF.

PANTRY

FOYER
8'-8" X 6'-2"
10' CEILING

SHWR

GLASS BLKS

WHP TUB

M.BATH
18'-10" X 12'-4"

UTIL CLS

LAU.
5'-0" X 6'-0"

GOLF CART

PORCH
8'-8" X 6'-2"
10' CEILING

8' COLUMN

BEDROOM 2
12'-0" X 11'-4"

OPT. VAULTED CEILING

GARAGE
19'-4" X 26'-10"

DINING RM.
12'-0" X 11'-2"

COVERED PORCH
17'-2" X 6'-4"

10' BOXED COLUMN

DESK

BAR

DW

KITCHEN
12'-0" X 13'-0"

GREAT ROOM
16'-10" X 15'-5"

OPT. 10' BOXED CEILING

8X8 BOXED COLUMN

MASTER SUITE
12'-10" X 14'-8"

OPT. 10' BOXED CEILING

REF.

PANTRY

FOYER
8'-8" X 6'-2"
10' CEILING

UTIL CLS

SHWR

WHP TUB

GLASS BLKS

M.BATH
18'-10" X 12'-4"

BEDROOM 2
12'-0" X 11'-4"

OPT. VAULTED CEILING

PORCH
8'-8" X 6'-2"
10' CEILING

8' BOXED COLUMN

W. LAU.
6'-0" X 6'-2"

GOLF CART

GARAGE
19'-4" X 26'-10"

PLAN DETAILS

- 1,536 total square feet of living area
- Living room joins the kitchen/dining area for an open atmosphere
- L-shaped kitchen with outdoor access and convenient laundry area
- Linen and coat closet
- Each unit has 2 bedrooms, 1 bath
- Crawl space foundation, drawings also include slab foundation
- Duplex has 768 total square feet of living space per unit

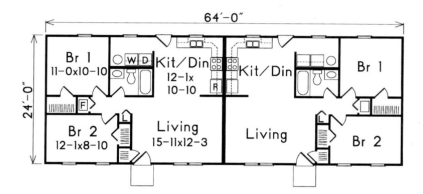

64'-0"

24'-0"

Br 1
11-0x10-10

W D

Kit/Din
12-1x
10-10

F

Br 2
12-1x8-10

Living
15-11x12-3

Kit/Din

R

Living

Br 1

Br 2

Rear View

PLAN DETAILS

- 7,372 total square feet of living area
- Units A and D include 3 bedrooms, 3 baths, 2-car garage in a ranch plan with 1,707 square feet of living area with 1,149 on the first floor and 558 on the lower level
- Units B and C include 3 bedrooms, 2 1/2 baths, 2-car garage in a two-story plan with 1,979 square feet of living area with 1,055 on the first floor and 924 on the second floor
- Basement foundation

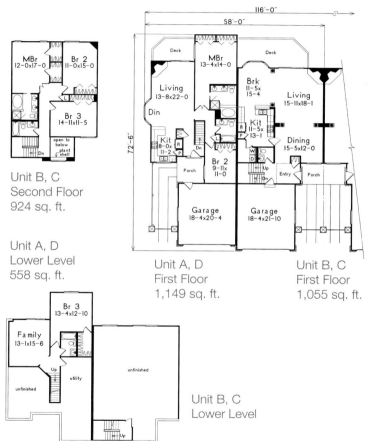

MBr 12-0x17-0

Br 2 11-0x15-0

Br 3 14-11x11-5

open to below

plant shelf

Dn

L

Unit B, C
Second Floor
924 sq. ft.

Unit A, D
Lower Level
558 sq. ft.

116'-0"

58'-0"

72'-6"

Deck

MBr 13-4x14-0

Deck

Living 13-8x22-0

Din

Kit 8-0x 11-2

R

P

Dn

Br 2 9-11x 11-0

Porch

Garage 18-4x20-4

Brk 11-5x 15-4

Kit 11-5x 13-1

R

L

P

W
D

Up

Dn

Entry

Living 15-11x18-1

Dining 15-5x12-0

Porch

Garage 18-4x21-10

Unit A, D
First Floor
1,149 sq. ft.

Unit B, C
First Floor
1,055 sq. ft.

Br 3 13-4x12-10

Family 13-1x15-6

Up

utility

unfinished

unfinished

unfinished

Up

Unit B, C
Lower Level

315

PLAN DETAILS

- 1,844 total square feet of living area
- Compact duplex design is ideal for a narrow lot in any neighborhood
- Spacious U-shaped kitchen includes a pantry and has plenty of room for dining
- Bedroom #2 is roomy and enjoys access to the rear patio which includes a storage closet
- Each unit has 2 bedrooms, 1 bath
- Slab or crawl space foundation, please specify when ordering
- Duplex has 922 square feet of living area per unit

37'-2"

56'-10"

PATIO
14'-0" X 5'-4"

STRG. STRG.

PATIO
14'-0" X 5'-4"

BEDROOM 2
17'-11" X 10'-0"

BEDROOM 2
17'-11" X 10'-0"

BEDROOM 1
11'-1" X 10'-0"

W

D

W

D

BEDROOM 1
11'-1" X 10'-0"

WH

WH

RG

RG

KITCHEN
17'-11" X 11'-6"

KITCHEN
17'-11" X 11'-6"

D.W

REF

PAN

REF

D.W

PAN

GREAT RM.
17'-11" X 13'-0"

GREAT RM.
17'-11" X 13'-0"

PORCH
11'-0" X 4'-8"

PORCH
11'-0" X 4'-8"

317

PLAN NUMBER: 586-038D-0072

PRICE CODE: F

PLAN DETAILS

- 2,860 total square feet of living area
- The elegant dining room is defined by arched entryways and is conveniently adjacent to the kitchen
- A box-bay window in the living area floods the space with natural light
- The master bedroom enjoys a walk-in closet and private bath with a double-bowl vanity
- Each unit has 3 bedrooms, 2 baths, 1-car garage
- Basement, slab or crawl space foundation, please specify when ordering
- Duplex has 1,430 square feet of living space per unit

Width: 84'-0"
Depth: 56'-8"

Mstr Br
13-5 x 14

Br 3
14-5 x 9-10

Br 2
12 x 10-5

Optional Deck

DN

DN

Kit
11x8-8

Living
12-11 x 19-5

SLOPE

ARCH

ARCH

13-5 x 23-11

Garage
13-5 x 21-11

ARCH

ARCH

Dining
10-1 x 12

ARCH

Rear View

PLAN DETAILS

- 2,406 total square feet of living area
- The front of each unit includes the great room and spacious kitchen with room for dining and entertaining
- The hallway leads to the private bedrooms and includes a convenient laundry closet
- Bedroom #3 enjoys a private bath, walk-in closet and access to the patio which includes a storage closet
- Each unit has 3 bedrooms, 2 baths
- Slab or crawl space foundation, please specify when ordering
- Duplex has 1,203 square feet of living area per unit

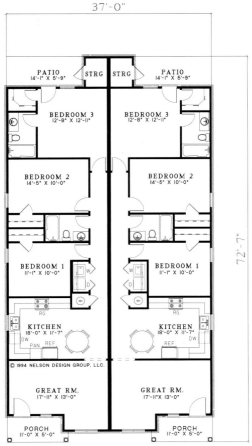

37'-0"

72'-7"

PATIO
14'-1" X 5'-9"

STRG STRG

PATIO
14'-1" X 5'-9"

BEDROOM 3
12'-8" X 12'-11"

BEDROOM 3
12'-8" X 12'-11"

BEDROOM 2
14'-5" X 10'-0"

BEDROOM 2
14'-5" X 10'-0"

BEDROOM 1
11'-1" X 10'-0"

BEDROOM 1
11'-1" X 10'-0"

W
D

W
D

KITCHEN
18'-0" X 11'-7"

RG

RG

KITCHEN
18'-0" X 11'-7"

DW

PAN REF

REF

DW

© 1994 NELSON DESIGN GROUP, LLC.

GREAT RM.
17'-11" X 13'-0"

GREAT RM.
17'-11" X 13'-0"

PORCH
11'-0" X 5'-0"

PORCH
11'-0" X 5'-0"

321

PLAN DETAILS

- 844 total square feet of living area
- Unique design with maximum privacy for each unit featuring its own porch, breezeway entrance and large sundeck
- Living room offers separate entry with closet, fireplace, sliding doors to deck and opens to dining area with bay window
- The bedroom features a private bath, closet and views to porch
- Each unit has 1 bedroom, 1 bath and a shared 2-car garage
- Crawl space foundation
- Duplex has 422 square feet of living area

322

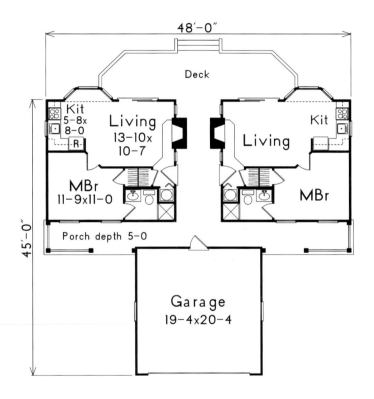

48'-0"

Deck

Kit
5-8x
8-0
R

Living
13-10x
10-7

Kit

Living

MBr
11-9x11-0

MBr

45'-0"

Porch depth 5-0

Garage
19-4x20-4

PLAN DETAILS

- 2,110 total square feet of living area
- Efficiently designed kitchen
- Formal dining room has an open feel with decorative columned wall
- Spacious living room has access to the covered grilling porch
- Each unit has 2 bedrooms, 2 baths
- Crawl space or slab foundation, please specify when ordering
- Duplex has 1,055 square feet of living space per unit

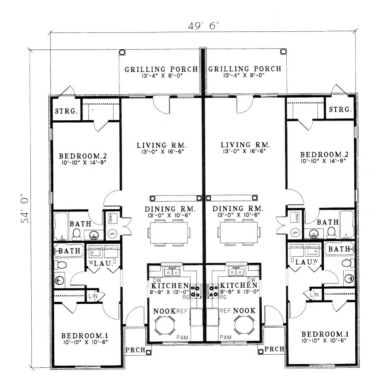

49' 6"

54' 0"

GRILLING PORCH
13'-4" X 8'-0"

GRILLING PORCH
13'-4" X 8'-0"

STRG.

LIVING RM.
13'-0" X 16'-6"

LIVING RM.
13'-0" X 16'-6"

STRG.

BEDROOM.2
10'-10" X 14'-9"

BEDROOM.2
10'-10" X 14'-9"

DINING RM.
13'-0" X 10'-6"

DINING RM.
13'-0" X 10'-6"

BATH

BATH

BATH

BATH

W LAU D

D LAU W

LIN

KITCHEN
8'-8" X 13'-0"

KITCHEN
8'-9" X 13'-0"

LIN

NOOK

NOOK

BEDROOM.1
10'-10" X 10'-6"

PRCH

PRCH

BEDROOM.1
10'-10" X 10'-6"

PLAN DETAILS

- 1,892 total square feet of living area
- Sliding door in kitchen for rear access
- Breakfast bar in kitchen overlooks dining and living areas
- Entry hall has closet for coats and extra storage
- Each unit has 2 bedrooms, 1 bath
- Basement foundation
- Duplex has 946 square feet of living space per unit

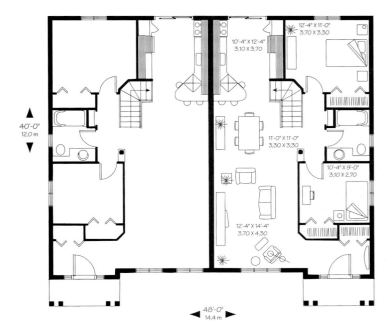

12'-4" X 11'-0"
3,70 X 3,30

10'-4" X 12'-4"
3,10 X 3,70

11'-0" X 11'-0"
3,30 X 3,30

10'-4" X 9'-0"
3,10 X 2,70

12'-4" X 14'-4"
3,70 X 4,30

40'-0"
12,0 m

48'-0"
14,4 m

327

PLAN DETAILS

- 6,410 total square feet of living area
- All master bedrooms have a private bath and walk-in closet
- Unit A has 1,962 square feet of living space with 3 bedrooms, 2 1/2 baths, 2-car garage
- Unit B has 1,471 square feet of living space with 2 bedrooms, 2 1/2 baths
- Unit C has 1,577 square feet of living space with 2 bedrooms, 2 1/2 baths, 1-car garage
- Unit D has 1,400 square feet of living space with 2 bedrooms, 2 baths, 1-car garage
- Slab foundation

Unit A
Second Floor
750 sq. ft.

Unit B
Second Floor
684 sq. ft.

Unit C
Second Floor
771 sq. ft.

Unit D
1,400 sq. ft.

Unit A
First Floor
1,212 sq. ft.

Unit B
First Floor
787 sq. ft.

Unit C
First Floor
806 sq. ft.

PLAN DETAILS

- 3,360 total square feet of living area
- Bedrooms have ample closet space
- Laundry closet is near both bedrooms
- Convenient U-shaped kitchen is adjacent to the dining room with access to the deck on the first floor and balcony on the second floor
- Adjacent to the living room is a handy coat and linen closet
- Each unit has 2 bedrooms, 1 bath
- Crawl space foundation, drawings also include slab foundation
- Fourplex has 840 square feet of living space per unit

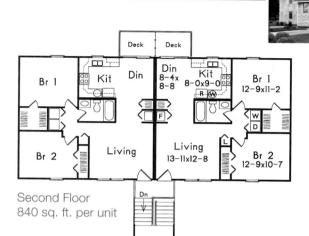

Second Floor
840 sq. ft. per unit

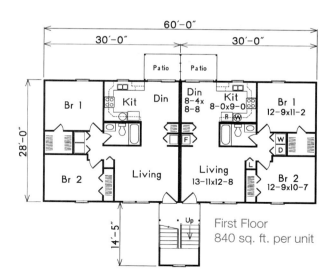

First Floor
840 sq. ft. per unit

PLAN DETAILS

- 1,704 total square feet of living area
- Smartly designed layout with emphasis on efficiency
- Functional kitchen embraces the sun with its bay window, glass sliding doors and pass-through to living room
- Five generously designed closets offer an abundance of storage
- Each unit has 2 bedrooms, 1 bath, 1-car garage
- Basement foundation
- Duplex has 852 square feet of living space per unit

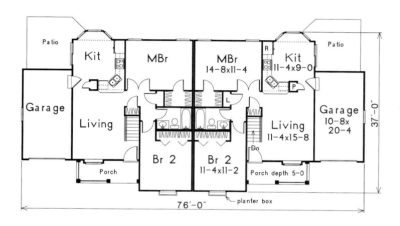

Patio

Kit

MBr

MBr
14-8x11-4

R

Kit
11-4x9-0

Patio

Garage

Living

L

P

Garage
10-8x
20-4

37'-0"

Br 2

Br 2
11-4x11-2

Dn

Living
11-4x15-8

Porch

Porch depth 5-0

planter box

76'-0"

Rear View

PLAN DETAILS

- 2,010 total square feet of living area
- The living areas include a spacious great room, half bath and efficient kitchen and dining area
- The bedrooms are located on the second floor for privacy
- Bedroom #1 features French doors leading to the second floor balcony
- Each unit has 2 bedrooms, 1 1/2 baths
- Basement or walk-out basement foundation, please specify when ordering
- Duplex has 1,005 square feet of living area per unit with 516 square feet on the first floor and 489 square feet on the second floor

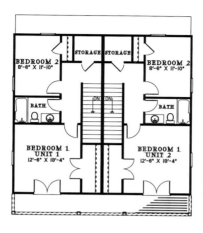

Second Floor
978 sq. ft.

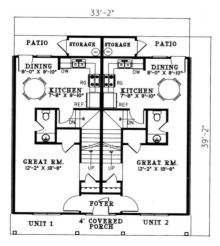

First Floor
1,032 sq. ft.

PLAN NUMBER: 586-059D-7507

PRICE CODE: P12

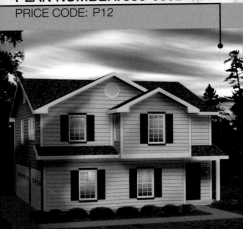

PLAN DETAILS

- 973 square feet
- Building height - 24'-8"
- Roof pitch - 6/12
- Ceiling height - 8'
- 2 bedrooms, 1 bath
- 9' x 7', 16' x 7' overhead doors
- Sunny breakfast room is positioned between the kitchen and the family room for convenience
- Complete list of materials

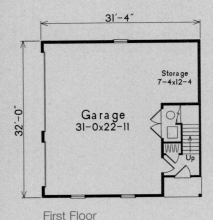

First Floor

Second Floor

PLAN DETAILS

- 566 square feet
- Building height - 22'
- Roof pitch - 4.5/12, 12/12
- Ceiling heights -
  First floor - 8'
  Second floor - 7'-7"
- Two 9' x 7' overhead doors
- Charming dormers add appeal to this design
- Complete list of materials
- Step-by-step instructions

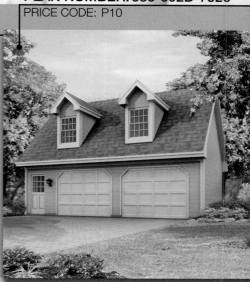

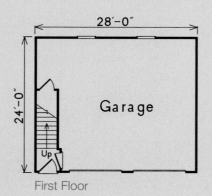

28'-0"

24'-0"

Garage

Up

First Floor

Dn

Studio
18-2x18-4

Second Floor

PLAN DETAILS

- 868 square feet
- Building height - 28'
- Roof pitch - 8/12, 10/12
- Ceiling heights -
    First floor - 9'
    Second floor - 8'
- 1 bedroom, 1 bath
- Two 9' x 7' overhead doors
- Large windows brighten the adjoining dining and great rooms
- Complete list of materials

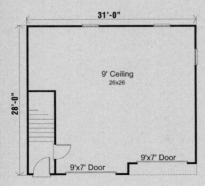

First Floor

31'-0"

28'-0"

9' Ceiling
26x26

9'x7' Door

9'x7' Door

Second Floor

Dining
13x10-4

Kitchen

Great Room
13x11

MBr.
12x10-9

PLAN DETAILS

- 654 square feet
- Building height - 24'
- Roof pitch - 7/12
- Ceiling height - 8'
- 16' x 7' overhead door
- 1 bedroom, 1 bath
- Vaulted living room is open to a pass-through kitchen and breakfast bar with an overhead plant shelf and sliding glass doors to an outdoor balcony
- Complete list of materials

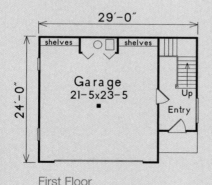

First Floor

29'-0"

24'-0"

shelves ○ □ shelves

Garage
21-5x23-5

Up

Entry

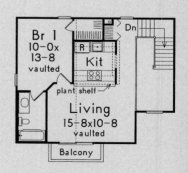

Second Floor

Br 1
10-0x
13-8
vaulted

Dn

Kit
R

plant shelf

Living
15-8x10-8
vaulted

Balcony

PLAN NUMBER: 586-063D-7504

PRICE CODE: P11

PLAN DETAILS

- 676 square feet
- Building height - 22'
- Roof pitch - 12/12
- Ceiling height - 8'
- 9' x 7', 16' x 7' overhead doors
- 1 bedroom, 1 bath
- L-shaped kitchen joins the living area to create an open feeling
- Complete list of materials

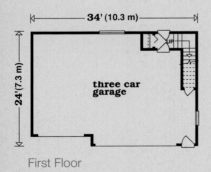

34' (10.3 m)

24' (7.3 m)

three car garage

First Floor

WIC

br
10'x12'

k
11'2x8'

DN

W D

HWT

liv
12'4x15'

Second Floor

PLAN DETAILS

- 576 square feet
- Building height - 21'-5"
- Roof pitch - 4/12
- Ceiling height - 8'
- Two 9' x 7' overhead doors
- 1 bedroom, 1 bath
- Loft has roomy kitchen and dining area
- Private side exterior entrance
- Complete list of materials
- Step-by-step instructions

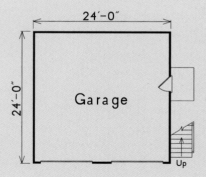

First Floor

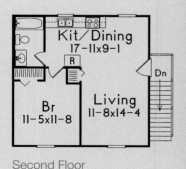

Second Floor

341

PLAN NUMBER: 586-009D-7502

PRICE CODE: P13

PLAN DETAILS

- 628 square feet
- Building height - 26'-6"
- Roof pitch - 8/12, 9/12
- Ceiling heights -
   First floor - 9'
   Second floor - 8'
- 16' x 7' overhead door
- 1 bedroom, 1 bath
- Cozy living room offers vaulted ceiling, fireplace and a pass-through kitchen
- Complete list of materials

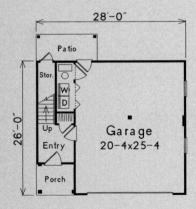

First Floor

28'-0"

26'-0"

Patio

Stor.

W / D

Up

Entry

Porch

Garage
20-4x25-4

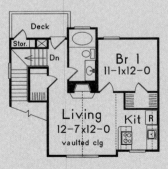

Second Floor

Deck

Stor.

Dn

Br 1
11-1x12-0

Living
12-7x12-0
vaulted clg

Kit
R

PLAN DETAILS

- 840 square feet
- Building height - 25'-8"
- Roof pitch - 7/12
- Ceiling heights -
    First floor - 9'
    Second floor - 8'
- 1 bedroom, 1 bath
- Two 9' x 7' overhead doors
- Cozy covered entry
- Complete list of materials

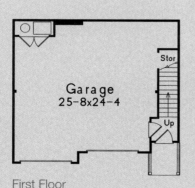

First Floor

Garage
25-8x24-4

Stor

Up

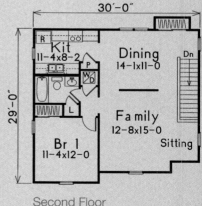

Second Floor

30'-0"

29'-0"

R

Kit
11-4x8-2

Dining
14-1x11-0

P

Dn

W
D

L

Br 1
11-4x12-0

Family
12-8x15-0

Sitting

PLAN DETAILS

- 902 square feet
- Building height - 27'-4"
- Roof pitch - 9/12
- Ceiling heights -
  First floor - 9'
  Second floor - 8'
- Two 9' x 8' overhead doors
- 1 bedroom, 1 bath
- Living room connects to an L-shaped kitchen with pantry and dining area/balcony
- Complete list of materials

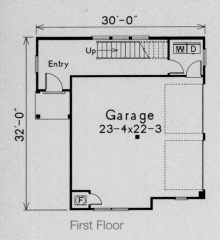

First Floor

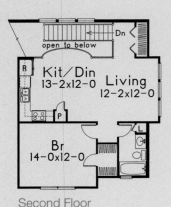

Second Floor

PLAN DETAILS

- 813 square feet
- Building height - 22'
- Roof pitch - 4.25/12, 12/12
- Ceiling height - 8'
- Three 9' x 7' overhead doors
- Studio, 1 bath
- Spacious studio apartment with kitchen and bath
- Complete list of materials

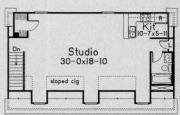

Second Floor

Kit
10-7x5-11

Studio
30-0x18-10

Dn

sloped clg

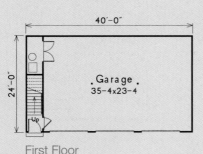

40'-0"

24'-0"

.Garage.
35-4x23-4

Up

First Floor

PLAN NUMBER: 586-009D-7504

PRICE CODE: P13

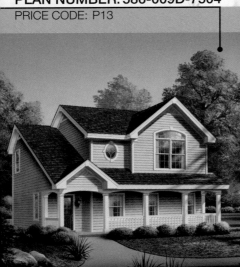

PLAN DETAILS

- 929 square feet
- Building height - 27'
- Roof pitch - 6.5/12, 10/12
- Ceiling heights -
  First floor - 9'
  Second floor - 8'
- 16' x 8', 9' x 8' overhead doors
- 2 bedrooms, 1 bath, 3-car side entry garage
- Living room has access to 8' x 12' deck
- Complete list of materials

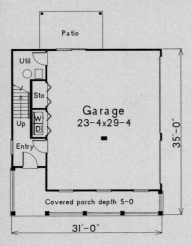

First Floor

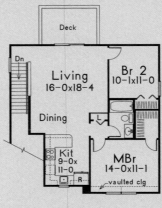

Second Floor

PLAN NUMBER: 586-059D-7506

PRICE CODE: P12

PLAN DETAILS

- 974 square feet
- Building height - 23'-2"
- Roof pitch - 5/12
- Ceiling height - 8'
- 2 bedrooms, 1 bath
- Three 9' x 7' overhead doors
- Efficiently designed kitchen and breakfast room combine with living area for spaciousness
- Complete list of materials

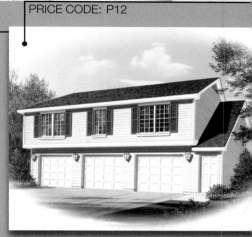

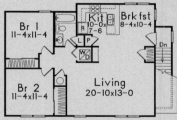

Second Floor

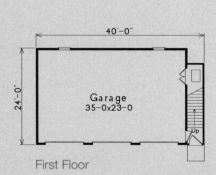

First Floor

PLAN NUMBER: 586-063D-7502

PRICE CODE: P11

PLAN DETAILS

- 588 square feet
- Building height - 23'
- Roof pitch - 4/12, 12/12
- Two 9' x 7' overhead doors
- Ceiling height - 8'
- 1 bedroom, 1 bath
- Charming dormers add character to exterior
- Convenient laundry space in kitchen
- Complete list of materials

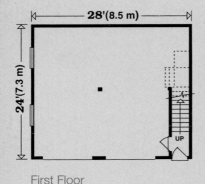

First Floor

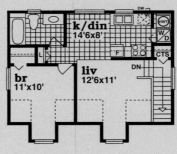

Second Floor

348

PLAN DETAILS

- 1,005 square feet
- Building height - 25'
- Roof pitch - 3.5/12, 6/12, 8/12
- Ceiling heights - First floor - 9' Second floor - 8'
- Three 9' x 8' overhead doors
- 2 bedrooms, 1 1/2 baths, 3-car garage
- Complete list of materials

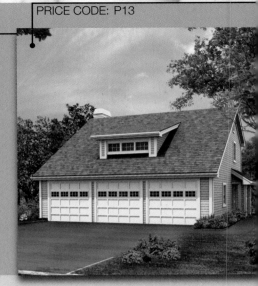

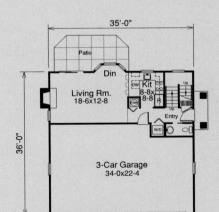

First Floor

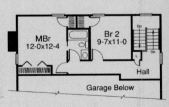

Second Floor

PLAN NUMBER: 586-009D-7508

PRICE CODE: P13

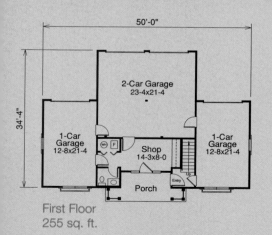

PLAN DETAILS

- 831 square feet
- Building height - 25'-6"
- Roof pitch - 10/12, 10.5/12
- Ceiling heights -
  First floor - 9'
  Second floor - 8'
- Four 9' x 8' overhead doors
- 1 bedroom, 1 1/2 baths
- Shop is 14'-3" x 8'-0" and includes built-in cabinets and toilet room
- Complete list of materials

First Floor
255 sq. ft.

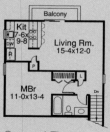

Second Floor
576 sq. ft.

PLAN DETAILS

- 1,032 square feet
- Building height - 24'
- Roof pitch - 5/12, 10/12
- Ceiling height - 8'
- 2 bedrooms, 1 bath
- Three 9' x 7' overhead doors
- Spacious family room flows into kitchen/ breakfast area
- Two sunny bedrooms share a bath
- Complete list of materials

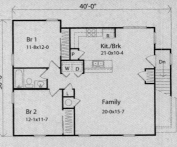

Second Floor

Br 1
11-8x12-0

Kit./Brk
21-0x10-4

Br 2
12-1x11-7

Family
20-0x15-7

40'-0"

30'-0"

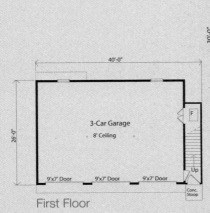

First Floor

3-Car Garage
8' Ceiling

40'-0"

26'-0"

9'x7' Door   9'x7' Door   9'x7' Door

Up

Conc. Stoop

Our Blueprint Packages Offer...

Quality plans for building your future,
with extras that provide unsurpassed value,
ensure good construction and long-term enjoyment.

Cover Sheet

Included with many of the plans, the
cover sheet is the artist's rendering of
the exterior of the home. It will give you
an idea of how your home will look when
completed and landscaped.

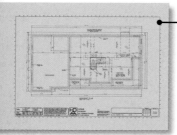

Foundation

The foundation plan shows the layout
of the basement, walk-out basement,
crawl space, slab or pier foundation. All
necessary notations and dimensions are
included. See plan page for the foundation types included. If the home plan
you choose does not have your desired
foundation type, our Customer Service
Representatives can advise you on how
to customize your foundation to suit your
specific needs or site conditions.

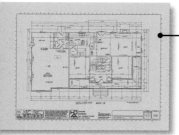

Floor Plans

The floor plans show the placement of
walls, doors, closets, plumbing fixtures,
electrical outlets, columns, and beams for
each level of the home.

Interior Elevations

Interior elevations provide views of special interior elements such as fireplaces, kitchen cabinets, built-in units and other features of the home.

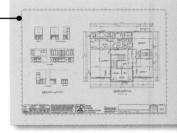

Exterior Elevations

Exterior elevations illustrate the front, rear and both sides of the house, with all details of exterior materials and the required dimensions.

Sections

Show detail views of the home or portions of the home as if it were sliced from the roof to the foundation. This sheet shows important areas such as load-bearing walls, stairs, joists, trusses and other structural elements, which are critical for proper construction.

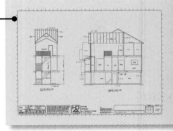

Details

Show how to construct certain components of your home, such as the roof system, stairs, deck, etc.

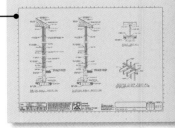

What kind of plan package do you need?

Once you find the home plan you've been looking for, here are some suggestions on how to make your Dream Home a reality. To get started, order the type of plans that fit your particular situation.

Your Choices:

THE 1-SET PACKAGE - We offer a 1-set plan package so you can study your home in detail. This one set is considered a study set and is marked "not for construction." It is a copyright violation to reproduce blueprints.

THE MINIMUM 5-SET PACKAGE - If you're ready to start the construction process, this 5-set package is the minimum number of blueprint sets you will need. It will require keeping close track of each set so they can be used by multiple subcontractors and tradespeople.

THE STANDARD 8-SET PACKAGE - For best results in terms of cost, schedule and quality of construction, we recommend you order eight (or more) sets of blueprints. Besides one set for yourself, additional sets of blueprints will be required by your mortgage lender, local building department, general contractor and all subcontractors working on foundation, electrical, plumbing, heating/air conditioning, carpentry work, etc.

REPRODUCIBLE MASTERS - If you wish to make some minor design changes, you'll want to order reproducible masters. These drawings contain the same information as the blueprints but are printed on erasable and reproducible paper which clearly indicates your right to copy or reproduce. This will allow your builder or a local design professional to make the necessary drawing changes without the major expense of redrawing the plans. This package also allows you to print copies of the modified plans as needed. The right of building only one structure from these plans is licensed exclusively to the buyer. You may not use this design to build a second or multiple dwellings without purchasing another blueprint. Each violation of the Copyright Law is punishable in a fine.

MIRROR REVERSE SETS - Plans can be printed in mirror reverse. These plans are useful when the house would fit your site better if all the rooms were on the opposite side than shown. They are simply a mirror image of the original drawings causing the lettering and dimensions to read backwards. Therefore, when ordering mirror reverse drawings, you must purchase at least one set of right-reading plans. Some of our plans are offered mirror reverse right-reading. This means the plan, lettering and dimensions are flipped but read correctly. See the Home Plans Index on pages 357-358 for availability.

Other great products...

The Legal Kit™ -

Avoid many legal pitfalls and build your home with confidence using the forms and contract featured in this kit. Included are request for proposal documents, various fixed price and cost plus contracts, instructions on how and when to use each form, warranty statements and more. Save time and money before you break ground on your new home or start a remodeling project. All forms are reproducible. The kit is ideal for homebuilders and contractors.
Cost: $35.00

Detail Plan Packages - Electrical, Plumbing and Framing Packages

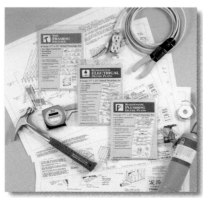

Three separate packages offer homebuilders details for constructing various foundations; numerous floor, wall and roof framing techniques; simple to complex residential wiring; sump and water softener hookups; plumbing connection methods; installation of septic systems, and more. Each package includes three dimensional illustrations and a glossary of terms. Purchase one or all three. Note: These drawings do not pertain to a specific home plan. **Cost: $20.00 each or all three for $40.00**

More helpful building aids

Your Blueprint Package contains the necessary construction information to build your home. We also offer the following products and services to save you time and money in the building process.

Express Delivery -

Most orders are processed within 24 hours of receipt. Please allow 7-10 business days for delivery. If you need to place a rush order, please call us by 11:00 a.m. Monday-Friday CST and ask for express service (allow 1-2 business days).

Technical Assistance -

If you have questions, please call our technical support line at 1-314-770-2228 between 8:00 a.m. and 5:00 p.m. Monday-Friday CST. Whether it involves design modifications or field assistance, our designers are extremely familiar with all of our designs and will be happy to help you. We want your home to be everything you expect it to be.

Material List -

Material lists are available for many of the plans in this publication. Each list gives you the quantity, dimensions and description of the building materials necessary to construct your home. You'll get faster and more accurate bids from your contractor while saving money by paying for only the materials you need. See the Home Plans Index on pages 357-358 for availability. Note: Material lists are not refundable. **Cost: $125.00**

Building Codes & Requirements

At the time the construction drawings were prepared, every effort was made to ensure that these plans and specifications meet nationally recognized codes. Our plans conform to most national building codes. Because building codes vary from area to area, some drawing modifications and/or the assistance of a professional designer or architect may be necessary to comply with your local codes or to accommodate specific building site conditions. We advise you to consult with your local building official for information regarding codes governing your area.

Home plans index

Plan Number	Square Feet	Price Code	Page	Material List	Right Read. Reverse	Can. Shipping	Plan Number	Square Feet	Price Code	Page	Material List	Right Read. Reverse	Can. Shipping
586-001D-0003	2,286	E	134	•			586-007D-0077	1,977	C	52	•		
586-001D-0013	1,882	D	68	•			586-007D-0091	3,502	H	268	•		
586-001D-0018	988	AA	190	•			586-007D-0092	2,901	G	282	•		
586-001D-0024	1,360	A	14	•			586-007D-0093	1,076	B	294	•		
586-001D-0027	2,328	D	122	•			586-007D-0094	2,408	F	308	•		
586-001D-0031	1,501	B	20	•			586-007D-0095	844	A	322	•		
586-001D-0036	1,320	A	80	•			586-007D-0096	2,986	G	218	•		
586-001D-0040	864	AAA	86	•			586-007D-0097	3,258	H	232	•		
586-001D-0067	1,285	B	56	•			586-007D-0098	2,397	D	46	•		
586-001D-0074	1,664	B	74	•			586-007D-0105	1,084	AA	170	•		
586-001D-0094	3,360	H	330	•			586-007D-0107	1,161	AA	192	•		
586-001D-0097	1,536	D	312	•			586-007D-0117	2,695	E	106	•		
586-001D-0098	1,536	D	296	•			586-007D-0118	1,991	C	118	•		
586-002D-7526	566	P10	337	x			586-007D-0140	1,591	B	150	•		
586-002D-7528	576	P9	341	x			586-007D-0150	2,420	D	204			
586-002D-7530	813	P12	345	x			586-007D-0155	2,636	E	164			
586-003D-0001	2,058	C	124	•			586-007D-0162	1,519	B	198			
586-003D-0002	1,676	B	168	•			586-007D-0164	1,741	B	156			
586-003D-0005	1,708	B	36	•			586-008D-0032	3,674	H	242			
586-004D-0001	2,505	D	78	•			586-008D-0034	3,648	H	256			
586-005D-0001	1,400	B	10	•			586-008D-0100	3,066	G	270	•		
586-006D-0003	1,674	B	90	•			586-009D-7500	654	P13	339	x		
586-007D-0001	2,597	E	94	•			586-009D-7502	628	P13	342	x		
586-007D-0010	1,721	C	16	•			586-009D-7504	929	P13	346	x		
586-007D-0019	1,700	D	214	•			586-009D-7505	902	P13	344	x		
586-007D-0020	2,318	F	224	•			586-009D-7508	831	P13	350	x		
586-007D-0021	2,840	G	240	•			586-009D-7509	1,005	P13	349	x		
586-007D-0022	4,240	H	272	•			586-010D-0006	1,170	AA	62	•		
586-007D-0023	7,372	H	314	•			586-013D-0015	1,787	B	38			•
586-007D-0024	2,986	G	300	•			586-013D-0019	1,992	C	96	•		•
586-007D-0025	1,992	E	246	•			586-013D-0022	1,992	C	6	•		•
586-007D-0026	1,704	D	332	•			586-013D-0025	2,097	C	44	•		•
586-007D-0030	1,140	AA	70	•			586-020D-0015	1,191	AA	64	•		
586-007D-0049	1,791	C	22	•			586-020D-0023	2,166	C	252			
586-007D-0054	1,575	B	58	•			586-020D-0038	1,770	B	130			
586-007D-0055	2,029	D	12	•			586-020D-0054	1,656	B	230			
586-007D-0060	1,268	B	28	•			586-021D-0007	1,868	D	104	•		
586-007D-0061	1,340	A	128	•			586-023D-0013	2,885	G	212	•		
586-007D-0062	2,483	D	88	•			586-023D-0014	4,184	H	220			
586-007D-0065	2,218	D	100	•			586-024D-0009	1,704	B	108			
586-007D-0066	2,408	D	138	•			586-024D-0064	2,391	E	184			
586-007D-0067	1,761	B	34	•			586-024D-0065	2,241	C	166			
586-007D-0068	1,384	B	40	•			586-025D-0061	5,516	H	234			
586-007D-0075	1,684	B	112	•			586-025D-0062	6,410	H	328			
586-007D-0076	3,666	H	254	•			586-025D-0063	4,131	H	260			

"**x**" indicates material list
included with plan purchase.

Home plans index

"x" indicates material list
included with plan purchase.

Important ordering information

How To Order:

1. **CALL** toll-free 1-800-373-2646 for credit card orders. MasterCard, Visa, Discover and American Express are accepted.

2. **FAX** your order to 1-314-770-2226.

3. **MAIL** the Order Form to: **HDA, Inc.**
   944 Anglum Road
   St. Louis, MO 63042

4. **ONLINE** visit www.houseplansandmore.com

Blueprint price schedule

BEST VALUE

Price Code	1-Set	SAVE $110 5-Sets	SAVE $200 8 Sets	Reproducible Masters
P9	$125	N/A	N/A	$200
P10	$150	N/A	N/A	$225
P11	$175	N/A	N/A	$250
P12	$200	N/A	N/A	$275
P13	$225	N/A	N/A	$440
AAA	$225	$295	$340	$440
AA	$325	$395	$440	$540
A	$385	$455	$500	$600
B	$445	$515	$560	$660
C	$500	$570	$615	$715
D	$560	$630	$675	$775
E	$620	$690	$735	$835
F	$675	$745	$790	$890
G	$765	$835	$880	$980
H	$890	$960	$1005	$1105

Shipping and handling charges

	1-4 Sets	5-7 Sets	8 Sets or Reproducibles
U.S. Shipping - (AK and HI express only)			
Regular (allow 7-10 business days)	$15.00	$17.50	$25.00
Priority (allow 3-5 business days)	$25.00	$30.00	$35.00
Express* (allow 1-2 business days)	$35.00	$40.00	$45.00
Canada Shipping** (to/from) - Plans with suffix 032D - see index			
Standard (allow 8-12 business days)	$35.00	$40.00	$45.00
Express* (allow 3-5 business days)	$80.00	$70.00	$80.00

* For express delivery please call us by 11:00 a.m. Monday-Friday CST

** Orders may be subject to custom's fees and or duties/taxes

Plan prices are subject to change without notice. Please note that plans and material lists are not refundable.

Exchange Policies - Since blueprints are printed in response to your order, we cannot honor requests for refunds. However, if for some reason you find that the plan you have purchased does not meet your requirements, you may exchange that plan for another plan in our collection within 90 days of purchase. At the time of the exchange, you will be charged a processing fee of 25% of your original plan package price, plus the difference in price between the plan packages (if applicable) and the cost to ship the new plans to you. Please note: Reproducible drawings can only be exchanged if the package is unopened.

Order form

Please send me -

PLAN NUMBER 586-_____ **PRICE CODE** _____ (see pages 357-358)

Specify Foundation Type (see plan page for availability)

☐ **Slab**   ☐ **Crawl space**   ☐ **Pier**   ☐ **Basement**   ☐ **Walk-out basement**

☐ **Reproducible Masters** $ _____

☐ **Eight-Set Plan Package** $ _____

☐ **Five-Set Plan Package** $ _____

☐ **One-Set Study Package** (no mirror reverse) $ _____

Additional Plan Sets*

   ☐ _____ (Qty.) at $20.00 each (price codes P9-P12) $ _____

   ☐ _____ (Qty.) at $45.00 each (price codes P13-H)

Mirror Reverse*

   ☐ Right-reading $150 one-time charge $ _____
      (see index on pages 357-358 for availability)

   ☐ Print in Mirror Reverse (where right-reading is not available)

      _____ (Qty.) at $15.00 each $ _____

☐ **Material List*** $125 (see pages 357-358 for availability) $ _____

☐ **Legal Kit** (see page 355) $ _____

Detail Plan Packages: (see page 355)

   ☐ Framing   ☐ Electrical   ☐ Plumbing $ _____

                                     SUBTOTAL $ _____

      Sales Tax (MO residents add 6%) $ _____

☐ Shipping / Handling (see page 359) $ _____

TOTAL (US funds only - sorry no CODs) $ _____

I hereby authorize HDA, Inc. to charge this purchase to my credit card account

☐ MasterCard   ☐ VISA   ☐ DISCOVER   ☐ Cards

Credit Card number _____

Expiration date _____

Signature _____

Name _____
                              (Please print or type)

Street Address _____
                        (Please DO NOT use a PO Box)

City _____

State _____ Zip _____

Daytime phone number (_____) - _____ - _____

E-mail address _____

   I'm a   ☐ Builder/Contractor   ☐ Homeowner   ☐ Renter

   I ☐ have ☐ have not selected my general contractor.

Questions?
Call Customer Service   360
1-314-770-2228   Thank you for your order!